Rio de Janeiro

Big City Food Biographies Series

Series Editor

Ken Albala, University of the Pacific, kalbala@pacific.edu

Food helps define the cultural identity of cities in much the same way as the distinctive architecture and famous personalities. Great cities have one-of-a-kind food cultures, offering the essence of the multitudes who have immigrated there and shaped foodways through time. The **Big City Food Biographies** series focuses on those metropolises celebrated as culinary destinations, with their iconic dishes, ethnic neighborhoods, markets, restaurants, and chefs. Guidebooks to cities abound, but these are real biographies that will satisfy readers' desire to know the full food culture of a city. Each narrative volume, devoted to a different city, explains the history, the natural resources, and the people that make that city's food culture unique. Each biography also looks at the markets, historic restaurants, signature dishes, and great cookbooks that are part of the city's gastronomic make-up.

Books in the Series

New Orleans: A Food Biography, by Elizabeth M. Williams

San Francisco: A Food Biography, by Erica J. Peters

New York City: A Food Biography, by Andrew F. Smith

Portland: A Food Biography, by Heather Arndt Anderson

Chicago: A Food Biography, by Daniel R. Block and Howard B. Rosing

Kansas City: A Food Biography, by Andrea L. Broomfield

Rio de Janeiro

A Food Biography

Marcia Zoladz

ROWMAN & LITTLEFIELD
Lanham • Boulder • New York • London

Published by Rowman & Littlefield
A wholly owned subsidiary of The Rowman & Littlefield Publishing Group, Inc.
4501 Forbes Boulevard, Suite 200, Lanham, Maryland 20706
www.rowman.com

Unit A, Whitacre Mews, 26-34 Stannary Street, London SE11 4AB

British Library Cataloguing in Publication Information Available

Library of Congress Cataloging-in-Publication Data

Names: Zoladz, Marcia, author.
Title: Rio de Janeiro : a food biography / Marcia Zoladz.
Description: Lanham : Rowman & Littlefield, [2016] | Series: The big city food biography series | Includes bibliographical references and index.
Identifiers: LCCN 2016010253 (print) | LCCN 2016025470 (ebook) | ISBN 9781442252318 (cloth : alk. paper) | ISBN 9781442252325 (Electronic)
Subjects: LCSH: Food—Brazil—Rio de Janeiro—History. | Restaurants—Brazil—Rio de Janeiro—Guidebooks. | Food industry and trade—Brazil—Rio de Janeiro—History. | Cooking—Brazil—Rio de Janeiro—History. | Rio de Janeiro (Brazil) —History.
Classification: LCC TX360.B73 R458 2016 (print) | LCC TX360.B73 (ebook) | DDC 394.1/2098153—dc23
LC record available at https://lccn.loc.gov/2016010253

Printed in the United States of America

Contents

Introduction

Rio de Janeiro is a city with well-known landmarks: Sugar Loaf, the Corcovado with the Christ statue at its top with its open arms, the beaches of Copacabana and Ipanema. It also has, though not so well known, the largest green area inside a city, the Tijuca Forest. It is also well known for its Carnaval with its pageants and celebrations and thousands of people singing and dancing in the streets of the city. It is a place full of enchantments. The soft rhythm of the bossa-nova, widely popularized by the "The Girl from Ipanema," for example, never lost its charm. This song—the music is by Antonio Carlos Jobim and the lyrics by Vinicius de Moraes—gave birth to the sound of a generation in the 1960s.

Less known, however, is the food in the city, which also is part of the history of its cultural development. The food that the local population hunted or foraged or farmed can be divided into three periods. In the first, when Amerindians and Europeans started to know each other in the sixteenth century, new foods, such as rice, sugarcane, chickens, and cattle were introduced by the Portuguese. At the same time, the Indigenous people taught the Europeans to eat cassava, to hunt the tapir, and to braise meat in a moquém, a small grill. In the second period, starting at the seventeenth century, the Portuguese brought enslaved Africans to work in sugarcane plantations and in the harbor of the city. A new adaptation process ensued with the introduction of recipes that steadily added sugar and salt, and cakes and stews unknown in the Amerindian kitchen were adopted. Using local ingredients, the settlers substituted for unavailable ones—peanuts instead of almonds, cassava flour instead of wheat flour—and introduced pumpkins, cooked beans, and the *Capsicum* pepper. The third and ongoing period began at the end of slavery in 1888, as a large number of immigrants from Europe and Levantine countries arrived, and their foods were added to the Afro-Portuguese list of recipes that already had absorbed Indigenous ingredients. Pizzas, kibbehs, and pastas were all as much a part of the local food repertoire as rice and black beans or small delicate pies.

The economic expansion in the Atlantic Ocean started in Portugal and Spain, the first countries to achieve central unified governments in Western Europe. Portugal had already expanded its dominion to the Madeira Islands, off the northwest coast of Africa, in 1419. They continued systematically exploring south, and crossed the continent's southernmost limit, the Cape of Good Hope, in 1497, gaining for a while a monopoly on the trade with Asia, the source of spices, especially black pepper, which made them quite rich.

The first Portuguese to arrive in today's Brazil declared the land the property of the Crown on April 22, 1500. The Church had granted the land to Portugal some years earlier, in an agreement between Portugal and Spain over the lands in the New World. The Treaty of Tordesillas, signed on June 7, 1494, divided all the lands of the world, those already known and the ones yet to be found, between Spain and Portugal. All lands east of the Tordesillas line were to belong to Portugal, and those to the west, to Spain, which included Columbus's discoveries. After Pedro Álvares Cabral arrived in Bahia and recognized the land as belonging to the Portuguese Crown, he took his fleet to India, as there was no special interest in the wilds of Brazil—yet.

There followed several expeditions in and around the region. The first one arrived on January 1, 1502. They thought the large bay that they entered was the estuary of a river, and named it Rio de Janeiro (January River); only later did they understand that they had arrived at the Bay of Guanabara. In passing through Rio, the first encounters with the local Amerindians and their food began. It was the first time Europeans confronted a society completely different from theirs.

For the first thirty years, the Portuguese only sent reconnaissance expeditions to the coast. The first traders of brazilwood (*Caesalpinia echinata*) then started to arrive. The original name of the tree, *Ibirapitanga* in Tupy, the language of the local population, means "red wood." *Brazil*, or rather *Ho Brasile*, is not a native word and it has no special meaning in Portuguese; rather, it is the Celtic name for an imaginary island located close to Ireland on medieval maps. The name meant "the Island of Fortune."

There is a map at the British Library by Grazioso Benincasa from 1473 that shows the island between England and Ireland. This island was a very important place in discussions of scholars in the fourteenth century about Paradise and whether it was located on Earth. It remained a theme in the years following Columbus's arrival in America.

Brazil had several names. The natives called it Pindorama, the land of the palm trees; the first Portuguese called it Island of Vera Cruz; in 1500, the name was Saint Cross for a while; and finally in 1527, Brazil. This name probably derived not from the trees but from those who traded in the red trees, who were called brasileiros (Brazilians).

The quantity of trees traded was large enough to give a general name of Brazilians to the whole population, and quite a few merchants were exchanging goods with the locals, the Portuguese, the Germans, and the French. This rhythm was disrupted in 1555 when the French established a colony in Rio, in the Bay of Guanabara. After they were expelled, the city was officially founded as São Sebastião do Rio de Janeiro, on January 21, 1565. But, before that, the influence of Rio in France was already felt. The French took several Amerindians back home to France and they started a French vogue of hats with strait plumes at the front of the head, called *à la sauvage*.

Apart from these small curiosities, a food biography of Rio brings the opportunity to discuss how a multicultural life established under adverse conditions could result in a rich vocabulary, built separately from the official colonial discourse, or because of the rebellions it caused. The food in the city was enormously influenced by the Africans arriving from the northeast of Brazil in the nineteenth century. Because of a slave revolt against the government in Bahia, the participants were deported and brought with them a completely new culinary tradition.

A food biography about Rio de Janeiro is an opportunity to unveil the high quality and variety of its fresh produce, the special dishes served at parties and at home, and the very traditional ones inherited from the immigrants that made the culture of the city as varied as its food.

Food for Cariocas—as those born in Rio are called—is uncomplicated, with straightforward flavors and long historical memories. It is very simple to cook, and yet Cariocas are always ready to come back home to eat codfish dumplings or rice and black beans sprinkled with a little bit of cassava flour. For those who have not tasted it, the different seasonings melt in the mouth and grow on the palate. The peppers from the *Capsicum* genus enhance the aromas and sharpen the taste of many dishes, it is hard to forget.

However, before making a specific list of the ingredients used in its dishes or describing and showing the regional recipes, there are some details that one should pay attention to for a better understanding of the food's qualities. From the beginning there has been a never-ending worry about the freshness of the food in Rio. The early difficulties of building the city in a tropical and unfamiliar part of the world imprinted the importance of the freshness of food in everybody's mind. Fresh food lessens the odds of contracting an illness. This begat a collective preoccupation that an ingredient had to be healthy, so dieting—not for losing weight but as guarantee of longevity—was indeed important.

Rio de Janeiro was plagued until the start of the twentieth century with yellow fever. Ships on their way to Argentina would not always stop at the harbor but remain outside the bay. Like all large cities, it had to deal with tuberculosis, measles, and other sicknesses as well. Until sulfa and antibiotics started to be prescribed on a large scale and vaccines were generalized, there was a constant fear that food could transmit disease. Therefore special care was taken in the way food was treated, and several recommendations were followed, such as never eat a raw salad outside the home, as one does not know the water that washed it. Only eat meat very well done, as rare meat can cause serious bowel problems. Fish must be fresh, otherwise it may be poisonous. There is common sense in this list, as on a hot day, even very fresh food can develop bacteria after sitting for a while on a kitchen counter.

Considered an important aspect of life during the nineteenth century, the concern for health at homes and in restaurants recalls the original cautious approach toward the unknown environment. Some traces of this discomfort with the tropics is noticeable in old recipe notebooks, where the recommendations about cooking methods and ingredients were quite justifiable. There were several recipes for purifying the blood that attest to the worry of the population about their health; common ingredients added to a meat broth were watercress and bitter almonds.

Today, many traditional dishes are still based in these old health notions. A fish soup is served with the pieces a little overcooked in traditional restaurants. Vegetables, fish, poultry, and meat are supposed to be fried in very hot oil or cooked in boiling water for a good twenty minutes. Well done or overdone food is often preferred in order to avoid a variety of tropical sicknesses. New chefs, however, do not follow these rules, as they are unnecessary in the modern era.

Cariocas have a dual perception of their city; on one hand, there is indeed a strong idea of their city as an idyllic place in a special landscape. And its 6.5 million inhabitants have a special cultural identity not directly linked to its public power. On the other hand, Rio is open to all and any foreign influence in food, as a rule, and each new addition is adapted to the Brazilian culture. American fast food, for instance, hamburgers and hot dogs, are associated with family meals and are loved by children, young adults, and adults when eating together. Moreover, when young adults and adults go out with friends, a more usual habit is to go to a bar or restaurant to drink an ice-cold beer or a *caipirinha*.

Rio's table is something unique, as food became associated with music as a political statement early in colonial times. Singers and dancers could stay for a long time near the street food stalls, and most of them were slaves; therefore, taking their time, as opposed to obeying their masters, was in a way an act of resistance against slavery.

View of the entrance of the Guanabara Bay with the Sugar Loaf on the right. *Source*: Marcia Zoladz.

The samba as a rhythm and as a cultural expression of the population began at the turn of the twentieth century when musicians gathered at a place called Pedra do Sal (the Salt Stone), the location of an ancient pier where ships with salt cargoes docked. There were several specialized landing places on the city shores; some were for coffee or grains, and there was a downtown fish market. Slaves arrived nearby at the Valongo Pier, the original arrival place of the African natives in the country.

European Romantic literature and painting of the nineteenth century emphasized the relation of humans with nature. This romantic perception of nature, however, was contemporary with another way of observing nature—the scientific approach of classifying every plant, animal, and ethnic group. In the end, both ways of representing the natural world stimulated a spa and health culture, developing habits such as sea bathing.

Today Rio de Janeiro still attracts photographers and contemporary artists to its inspiring geography. There is an enormous contrast between what the first inhabitants wanted in the city compared to contemporary expectations, even when this charm is almost a cliché of sun, sports, and gorgeous nightlife.

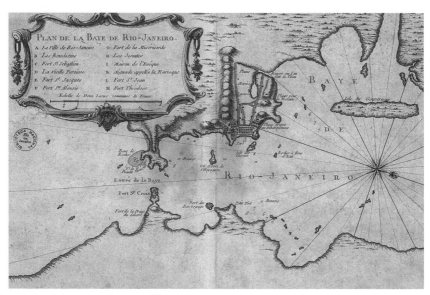

A carefully rendered map of the Guanabara Bay, by French cartographer Jacques-Nicollas Bellin, 1764. Notice the small and protected entrance. *Source*: Original map at the Fundação Biblioteca Nacional, http://www.wdl.org/en/item/187/.

Chapter One

The Material Resources

Land, Water, and Air

Facing the Atlantic Ocean and featuring two of the most famous mountains in the world, Rio de Janeiro has an impressive landscape. The Corcovado, with its profile high up against the sky, is crowned by the Christ the Redeemer statue. The statue opened to the public in 1931, although it was possible to visit the top of the mountain to enjoy the view since early in the nineteenth century by horse and via a small train service since 1885. The second mountain, the Sugar Loaf, also of world fame, is at the entrance of the Bay of Guanabara.

A tropical city located 22°54' 24" south of the equator, and 43°10' 21" west of the Greenwich meridian, Rio de Janeiro encompasses 1,255 square kilometers (486 square miles), and looking at its map, it is a long shoreline interrupted by a series of mountain chains. The Tijuca Massif, with its most famous mountain being the Corcovado, 710 meters (2,329 feet) high, gently slopes down to the east until it reaches the calm waters of the Bay of Guanabara. The bay covers 412 square kilometers (159 square miles), and its relatively small entrance protects its waters from tropical winds. Looking from the open sea, it is flanked on its left side by Sugar Loaf Mountain, 396 meters high (1,299 feet). There are two smaller elevations besides Sugar Loaf. Cara de Cão (Dog Face) and Morro do Leme (Rudder Mount), which signals the approach to the entrance of the bay for those coming from the south. On the other side, the bay is equally protected by another group of mountains. The Pico Mount protects the entrance in a symmetric position to the Sugar Loaf; these mountains are, however, part of the city across the bay from Rio, Niterói, which is as old as Rio. To make the approach into the entrance of the bay more difficult there is an island in the middle, Lage, a stone slab surfacing from the sea.

In the south, the city shoreline is bathed by the Atlantic Ocean, with beaches of white and fluffy sand. Copacabana, Ipanema, and Leblon are the famous ones, but with a coast 246.22 kilometers (153 miles) long, the sea acquires different nuances as it reaches the land, and the variations of its contour also influence the tide direction and the strength of the waves as they hit the beaches. Sometimes, more protected basins have smoother waters; others face the open sea and the surf arrives with high perfectly rounded swells and stronger currents.

The city today still has four inner lagoons. There were more, but over its history of four hundred fifty years, they became contaminated, and at the end of the nineteenth century, they were filled in for sanitary reasons during an enormous urbanization reform. French promenades and English gardens had been built over their waters. One of the lagoons, Lagoa Rodrigo de Freitas, in the south, however, did survive, in part because its location was in a rural and forested area, and also because of a canal linking its water with the Atlantic at the junction of Ipanema and Leblon beaches. At the start of the nineteenth century, this lagoon was not a densely populated area, although it had many activities around its shores, mostly farms, and it was far enough from the city center for the Crown to consider the region safe enough to establish a gunpowder factory in 1808. In the case of an attack by enemies, there would be enough ammunition outside the city center for the army. In the same year, the botanical garden of Rio de Janeiro was founded on the shores of the lagoon to adapt foreign species in the country.

The other four lagoons are also parallel to the sea, from east to west, Marapendi, Tijuca, Camorim, and Jacarepaguá, today are integrated in an existing mangrove vegetation protection zone in the central plains of the city. *Jacarepaguá*—the name in Tupy means a place full of alligators—named the whole region. This region was very important until the last cycle of colonial business at the end of the eighteenth century. Located in the flatlands, covering 160 square kilometers (61.77 square miles), it went through all the colonial commodities cycles. At first there were sugarcane plantations for the production of sugar and cattle ranches at the same time—the leather was used to make the boxes in which the sugar loaves were exported—cotton, and indigo (*anil* in Portuguese). Some of the region converted to coffee, and then, it was vegetables and farming until, in the last twenty-five years of the twentieth century, a new expansion and urbanization movement divided the land in the Jacarepaguá plains.

The large areas of Jacarepaguá and its surrounding mountains had easy access to the Bay of Guanabara, located to its northeast or to the Bay of Sepetiba to the west. A well-irrigated flat land below the region of the Pedra

Branca Mountains was also adequate for the development of the sugarcane plants.

Parallel to the lagoons, but retreating from the shore toward the northwestern region of the city there is a central mountain chain named after its highest peak, Pedra Branca, 1,024 meters (3,359.58 feet) high. Even farther north at the frontier another chain of mountains, Serra do Medanha, leads to the inland roads toward the State of Rio de Janeiro and the surrounding cities.

The western limits of the city lands surround the Bay of Sepetiba, an expanse of 305 square kilometers (117 square miles). The bay is protected from the Atlantic Ocean by a key forty-two kilometers (twenty-six miles) long, Restinga de Marambaia. Smaller than the Bay of Guanabara where the colonial enterprise started and developed from the sixteenth century, the bay developed a complementary local life with small towns around its waters; a hinterland not only with sugarcane plantations but also with many farms served as the entrance road for the cattle arriving from the south of the country. The bay had a small port used to transport local merchandise to the harbor at Guanabara Bay.

The economic activities of this area are mainly fishing and agriculture. It is in many ways still considered the other side of the city; its flat landscape surrounding the central mountain chain was more adequate for developing sugarcane, cotton, indigo, and the horticultural belt around the urbanized area, the center of the economic activity. It is quite far from the Bay of Guanabara a distance of sixty kilometers (37.28 miles).

CLIMATE AND VEGETATION

The climate is very hot and humid during the summer, from December to March. Temperatures are higher than 113 degrees Fahrenheit, with strong tropical rains. In winter, the lowest temperatures vary from 64.4 to 50 degrees Fahrenheit. Winter, from June to September in the Southern Hemisphere, is the dry season. Tropical flora in this latitude also varies according to altitude. At sea level, close to the beaches where the soil is sandy and with high salt content, low growth proliferates, changing into mangrove vegetation in the wetlands close to the lagoons. Near the foot of the mountains, the land profits from the rich sediments deposited by rivers and rainwater. The altitude variations in the relief, a combination of higher peaks, mounts, small hills, and flatlands, result in the typical flora variety of the Tijuca Forest in this latitude. Today, more than twenty thousand plant species live in the Forest, and eight thousand are indigenous.[1]

The Tijuca Forest system counterbalances the strong heat of the region, collaborating in the maintenance of the temperatures around the year in the city. The forest is a huge canopy system of larger trees projecting their shadows over other plants and keeping the moisture from escaping the soil. This extremely humid microclimate stimulated the growth of a large variety of species together, sometimes entangled one to another. It is a prolific mix of fruit-bearing trees, trees that are known for the beauty of their wood, and plants that are hosted by other plants—gigantic philodendra or tiny orchids, bromeliad, climbers, palm trees, all near each other but at the same time positioned according to their needs for more shadow, light, heat, or water from the soil.

The local vegetation was well understood by the Amerindians. Corn, arriving in Brazil in a natural migration from the Andes in prehistoric times, although not the staple of their diet, was also part of their nourishment together with native peanut (*Arachis hypogaea*), cassava, pepper, beans, yams, and heart of palm extracted from the *juçara* palm tree (*Euterpe edulis*). There are a large number of various fruit-bearing native trees, such as cashews, passion fruit, and jaboticaba—Brazilian grape tree (*Plinia cauliflora*), bearing dark blue almost black fruits with a sweet white pulp that grow directly from the trunk of the tree. There are guavas, *pitanga* (Brazilian cherry [*Eugenia uniflora*]), and *caraguatá* (*Bromelia antiachanta Bertol*) from the same family as pineapples but smaller and very acidic, which today is a decorative garden plant. There are the native nuts from the Tijuca Forest too, such as *sapucaia* (*Lecythidaceae*), from the same family as Brazil nuts, and Aroeira (*Schinus terebinthifolius*), pink peppercorns, a native from southeast and southern Brazil.

There are some doubts about the local origin of the *pacova* (*Musa paradisiaca*); they are the same kind of fruit as the African banana, but it is impossible to date their introduction in the country. Although early literature mention Amerindians peeling them like figs before eating, *pacovas*, called *bananas da terra* (bananas of the land) were probably introduced in the country early in the sixteenth century and acquired the Amerindian name *pacova*. The name means "plant used for packing," which is exactly the use they made of their large leaves, in which they carried food. Bananas are first mentioned in 1550, brought to the country, according to the reports of the Frenchman Jean de Léry; the Portuguese bananas were brought to Brazil from Africa by Portuguese who lived in the military bases of Cabo Frio in Rio de Janeiro and Igarassu in Pernambuco, in 1550.[2]

Not all the fruits and vegetables of the Tijuca Forest are native or arrived in prehistoric times. Two species introduced in the second half of the eighteenth century readily integrated into the landscape with the native fruits—mangoes and jackfruits. Mango (*Mangifera indica*) was brought to Brazil from Goa, where the Portuguese had a colony, the fruit with its yellow pulp is well beloved, eaten thinly sliced or in desserts, ice creams, and sorbets. Jack trees (*Artocarpus heterophyllus*) arrived at the same time, also from India, and had a similar adaptation process, its trunks with huge heavy fruits are found in parks and in the forest inside the city.

Geography defined where the first groups to arrive established themselves before, during, and after the colonial period. Rio inhabitants settled first in its protected areas around the mountains, close to the calm waters of the Bay of Guanabara toward its northern region and the Serra do Mar, a 1,500 kilometers (932 miles) long mountain system along the southeastern coast of Brazil.

Once colonial business started, an intense search for new products around the country followed, as they had a list of products of commercial value they were looking for based on the Portuguese experience in India. Fine woods were first on the list, as the Bay of Guanabara was in such a dense forest and brazilwood was readily available. A huge tree, pau-brazil (*Caesalphinia echinata*)—brazilwood—was valued for the red color of its trunk. There were other indigenous trees valued in Europe for their color by cabinetmakers and for their hardness; they were used for window casings and floors: jacarandá (*Fabacea*) and rosewood, or *peroba-rosa* (*Aspidosperma polyneuron*). Not all came from the Tijuca Forest around Rio; mahogany arrived from the northeast, also mahogany from Madeira was introduced in Brazil and exported.

The extraction of plants and crops were the first businesses in the city, as the region did not have any readily available mines, neither gold nor silver, as in Spanish America. The second economic cycle in the city was a longer one, and it defined for many centuries the land occupation and later its urban development.

Sugarcane arrived in Rio at the start of the seventeenth century and stayed until the nineteenth century, replaced by coffee farms. Sugarcane (*Saccharum officinalis*) is a tall grass used to produce sugar because of the high glucose content of the sap in its stems. In colonial times, after its extraction, the liquid was heated until it turned into a dark dense syrup, molasses, and was then divided into molds with a conical shape, where they would cool down and crystallize. The result were hard pieces of sugar called loaves, approximately 2 kilograms (4 pounds) each.

When the Portuguese started their maritime expansion in the Atlantic Ocean, sugarcane had already been adopted in Portugal. In the fifteenth century, they started the plantation system based on slave work in Madeira and Azores islands. One century later, when they expanded it to Brazil, they already had a good deal of experience as plantation owners, sugar producers, and international traders.

Sugar production on a large scale consumes a tremendous amount of coal and wood to keep the sweet sap boiling during the harvest; therefore, the central plains in Rio de Janeiro, at the bottom of the Tijuca Forest, became the place they chose to start their first mills. There were also sugarcane farms around the Bay of Guanabara. Sugarcane plantations were self-contained production units, comprising the farms, a sugar-processing mill, houses, stables, tool workshops, a vegetable garden, and all the facilities to house a large number of people. Sugarcane farms and the production of sugar introduced slave work in the country.

The other native crops inside the city were tobacco, cotton, and indigo, located in the same central plains as the sugar plantations, they profited from the same waterways, the internal lagoons and rivers, from where they were sent to the port in Sepetiba. Produce could also be sent by road to the Bay of Guanabara. The soil was not very adequate for either tobacco or cotton; later, these crops migrated to more productive areas in the country. Indigo was supplanted at the start of the nineteenth century by the crops from India, and their land was used to plant coffee.

COFFEE PLANTATIONS IN THE CITY

Coffee plants were at first disseminated in backyards in downtown Rio in 1760. Soon plantations spread from the central and the flat lands of the city to the higher terrains in the central area of the city in the Tijuca Forest. The coffee trees were planted in a straight line from the top to the bottom of the mountains, and although it might have seemed a logical solution at the time, it was the worst possible choice, as rains were constantly washing the soil of all its valuable nutrients. Coffee plants thrive in higher altitudes, but they need to be set in such a way that each row of trees is capable of retaining enough water and nutrients for itself, in small flat areas.

Because of the quick erosion of the soil, coffee plantations during the nineteenth century were constantly migrating. Exploration started by clearing an area, and, as the plants exhausted the nutrients, the plantation owner started another one in a newly "opened" farm. Cattle ranchers used the exhausted areas for grazing, which did not help much, as pasture grasses did not bring enough of the necessary composites to bring the forest to life again, and the trampling of the herds also crushed water springs in the fields.

The intense deforestation diminished the water supply in Rio. In order to keep and protect its water sources the government started a reforestation program in 1861, which was closely followed until 1888. Left alone, with designated visitation areas that included resting places, restaurants, and waterfalls, the original forest recuperated.

Coffee was already an appreciated beverage in Europe when the production expanded in the city. By 1675 there were more than three thousand coffee houses in England. Coffee farms started in Rio early in the nineteenth century; from 1817 to 1819, the port exported 211,547 bags of coffee grains (75 kg each). The coffee plantations expanded to the whole state of Rio de Janeiro and the state of Minas Gerais.

The port exported 14,734,797 bags (60 kg each) in 1865–1869. Because of predatory use of the soil, coffee production moved south, and the port only shipped 8,049,719 bags (60 kg) in 1870–1872, whereas the port of Santos, in the state of São Paulo, shipped 15,755,683 bags (60 kg) in the same period. Brazil today is the largest coffee producer in the world; the majority of the large producing farms are located in the state of São Paulo and in the north of the state of Paraná.[3]

THE WATER AND THE FISH OF THE CITY

The large expanse of the Tijuca Forest with its closeness to the sea meant the city had many of its rivers and streams located in intertidal zones, and as the population grew, deforestation and the leveling of smaller mounts to flatten the land for new buildings destroyed or polluted several drinking water sources. The solution for the constant lack of clean drinking water for the population and for supplying the ships was solved in 1750, when the government built a huge aqueduct of Roman dimensions right in the center of the urban area (270 meters long by 17.6 high). Built to bring fresh water from the mountains to the city, it ended in a central fountain, and from there the clean water was distributed through a system of fountains until it reached the harbor. The water supply and its pollution were a constant preoccupation of the authorities, and trying to protect the rivers' margins was a constant worry. The Carioca River, which supplied the aqueduct with part of its water, followed its course despite legislation to protect bananas plantations through Ascriego and its margins and obligations to keep the original vegetation there. Legislation to protect the water sources continued throughout the nineteenth century to control the use of its water and keep it clean.

The Tijuca Forest is larger than the area it occupies, extending its influence from the top of its mountains through the different vegetation zones, until it reaches the maritime platform. This influences the reproduction and preservation of many fish species, as several of them start their lives in the tide zones and swim toward the sea as they grow or feed in the intertidal areas and go back to sea.

The following are examples of the fish influenced by the forest. Not all are immediately edible, and there is a tendency today to enlarge the number of protected species. One such example on the Brazilian coast is the merou (*Epinephelus marginatus*), a fish that lives, like the grouper, close to the stones at the bottom of the sea, but is much larger reaching 250 kilograms (500 pounds), sometimes more. Corvines (*Micropongias furnieri*) also feed in the mangroves and close to river estuaries before they move to the open sea. Sardines (*Sardinella brasiliensis*) are very common on the coast, and have their stocks controlled by the government. Another fish that is quite appreciated is *pescada branca*, or hake (*Cynoscion leiarchus*), a common fish from South America with a white and flaky meat.

The fish offered in markets are either from the maritime platform—there is a two-hundred-mile commercial protection area where only Brazilian boats can fish, quite a large quantity are brought from regions as far away as Cabo Frio, in the north of the city—or from fish, oyster, and shrimp farms in the state of Santa Catarina. The majority of the lobsters arrive from the northeastern states.

The green turtle (*Chelonia midas*) can grow up to 120 centimeters (4 feet) long and weigh at maturity 300 kilograms (600 pounds). Turtles are under protection nowadays, but they used to be prepared as soup or braised; there were even restaurants where they were served as a specialty. The large southern right whale used to come to the Bay of Guanabara during winter. The oil extracted from their meat was very valuable; it was used in lamps instead of candles and in the construction of houses as an ingredient in an early cement. It was a strong binder added to the mixture of stones and sand. The meat was thrown away. Whaling has been forbidden in Brazil since 1985, and the coast is a protection zone for dolphins and whales.

The Boto-cinza—gray dolphin (*Sotalia guianensis*) immortalized in the coat of arms of the city, can be seen in the bay or from the beaches close to the coast, surfing the waves and following boats. They were not seen for a while when pollution and over fishing almost led to their disappearance, but now they are starting to come back. Their presence was quite common in the waters of Copacabana beach close to the large swells.

A SECRET DOOR TO THE CITY:
THE USE OF THE LAND AND THE WATER

Today the city is best known as a holiday alternative for Brazilians and visitors from all over the world, its vast coast and beaches are a constant attraction with full free access to the public. It was not always so. The sea, especially the open sea with large waves, tide variations, and strong currents, was a very menacing prospect for a city dweller. It was a door to pirates or hurricanes and tempests; therefore, early urban developers preferred to look inland, avoiding direct access to the open sea beaches.

Rio de Janeiro's steep mountains protect its mostly central flatlands, where the plantations had settled, and they were its real richness. The open sea was until the twentieth century used mainly for fishing and was a site for battles against invaders; the Atlantic Ocean with its free-roaming corsairs and pirates and its open sea beaches was a very impractical and unsafe place to build unprotected roads or farms.

The city only started to grow toward its southern region on the Atlantic Ocean after World War I, even if bathing in seawater was already considered very healthy in the early nineteenth century and the very calm and clean waters of the Bay of Guanabara were considered ideal. After three centuries of activity, the old buildings in the center of the city, located around the bay, had very few private houses, mostly commercial and industrial activities, and the city started to expand into the old farming areas.

As new immigrants started to arrive, the city had to expand its territory; there were 811,433 inhabitants recorded in the census of 1900.[4] The city then started its expansion toward its open sea beaches with white sands—Copacabana, Ipanema, and Leblon. The main access to several of the neighborhoods close to the sea was first the small roads through the mountains; only later did tunnels make the access easier, avoiding the shores. It is worth visiting the countryside here too, so different from the usual postcard images one sees.

As the population grew, especially after the end of the nineteenth century, a green belt replaced the plantation system based on slave work. Orchards and small properties were sometimes large enough for their produce to be sold at local markets; some were used for vacations and weekends, being only large enough to supply the families of their owners with vegetables and eggs.

In the west and the north of the city, farms were divided into suburban neighborhoods and farmsteads with names reminiscent of the original use of the land. Anil—indigo in Portuguese—was where the plantations were located. Campo Grande—it means "large field"—was from colonial times a resting area for cattle arriving from outside the city, as opposed to Campinho—"little field"—in the same region. As the city grew in importance and population, a horticultural belt developed in the state of Rio de Janeiro and in the surrounding states that still today provide fresh vegetables, fruit, and meat to the city.

With the urbanization of the southern region and its open sea beaches, occupation accelerated, and the first tunnel opened in 1892, linking the inland neighborhood of Botafogo to Copacabana, with its now famous beach. There, on the south, at the bottom of Corcovado Mountain, it was mostly farms. A military garrison with its installations, including a gunpowder factory, occupied the area close to sea, in *Leblon* and the *Lagoa Rodrigo de Freitas*, the large saltwater lagoon separated by an isthmus from the open sea beaches. The region was so far from the original urban population that there were a few *quilombos*, small villages of Africans, important bastions of survival and political resistance to slavery. There were roads crossing the mountains, even if the terrain was abrupt and difficult, but the open sea with its large waves was not a practical option for a regular transportation system like the one on the calm waters of the Bay of Guanabara. There is only a ferry system to link Rio with the city of Niterói, and to Paquetá, a small island farther inside the bay.

Chapter Two

Food in a Carioca Way

The First Inhabitants

Minha terra tem palmeiras,
Onde canta o sabiá.
As aves que aqui gorjeiam
Não gorjeiam como lá.

My land has palm trees
Where the thrush sings.
The birds that here sing
Do not sing as they do there.

—from "Song of Exile," by Gonçalves Dias, 1843

BEFORE THE AMERINDIAN ARRIVED

The earliest inhabitants of the coast of Rio de Janeiro arrived approximately six thousand years ago. They foraged; hunted small animals; and took mussels, oysters, and different kinds of shellfish from the sea, which they cooked in small fires. They disposed of the shells and bones in the same places they buried their dead. Archaeological excavations have discovered that they likewise put the remains of small animals they hunted, such as turtles, monkeys and other mammals, and small fishes in these places. Cassava plant fossils have also been uncovered, suggesting incipient agriculture. After a while, all these remains, solidly stacked with shells, formed mounds, and as they dissolved with the passing of time, their high lime content preserved all their contents. Judging by the locations of the shell mounds, these groups lived in an area stretching from the north of the State of Rio de Janeiro to the south of the State of Rio Grande do Sul, in Brazil. The next inhabitants of the region,

11

the Tupi, called them *sambaquis* (shell deposits). They were sedentary people who settled in small groups, and became known as *sambaqui* people.

Ceramic pots were recovered at some of the shell mounds, and although there is no proof the sambaqui culture produced kilns or were potters, these indicate that there might have been occasional contacts with other groups from inland. Archaeologists also uncovered stone figures in these deposits. Today it is known that they lived at sites in modern-day downtown Rio, as archaeological finds in the harbor zone tell their whereabouts inside the city; unfortunately, over the centuries many were excavated for their lime deposits.

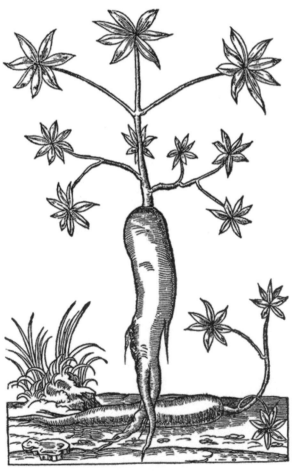

One of the first detailed illustrations of the cassava plant, from 1557. *Source*: André Thevét, *Les singularitez de la France Antarctique*, https://commons.wikimedia.org/wiki/File:Manihot_Thevet_1557_114r.png.

The Amerindian groups that the Europeans encountered when they arrived in Rio had settled in the area much later than the sambaqui people, approximately two thousand years ago, having moved out of the Amazon River basin, from the north. Instead of settling along the shores, they spread like a fan, establishing themselves from the coast inland to central Brazil.

These new arrivals were potters, and they knew fire and how to use it to create ceramic pans in which to cook food; the pans were placed on three stones set over the fire. Fire also had magical purposes, used for speaking with the spirits, understanding and healing a sickness, and lighting a pipe of tobacco in a ceremony. In addition, it was a very powerful weapon used to scare their enemies. When enemies where captured they were sacrificed in cannibalistic rituals.

The two Amerindian peoples around the Guanabara Bay were the *Tupinambás* and the *Temininós*. They lived around the bay in well-positioned villages from which they could watch the entrance of the bay or on islands well offshore. Knowledge about these groups has accumulated over the centuries, starting with the first contacts with Europeans and later sixteenth- and seventeenth-century reports. Gaps about their life in the archaeological record are filled by interpolations of similar habits of other groups around this area; implements found at archaeological excavation sites; or ad hoc finds at construction sites, private collections started in the nineteenth century, and public collections. It is from these that one learns that the quality of their ceramic was not very refined, but it was richly decorated, according to archaeologist Maria Beltrão.[1]

Brazil has a long tradition in ethnology beginning in 1808 with the Royal Museum in Rio de Janeiro, and before that with the many objects that were taken to Europe where they survive in national collections. Therefore, a cumulative knowledge has helped to build a rich image of who the Tupinambá and the other groups around them were. Together with the vestiges of their material culture, there is their food legacy in the reports about the preparation of fruits, vegetables, roots, and animals of the Atlantic Forest both by contemporary travelers and by the maintenance of these in the cuisine of Rio's population today.

The travelers' reports, because they were confronting a new world, sometimes include a little more than just a list of items in the region; they tell how the natives behaved, if they were friendly, if they liked the taste of European foods or not, and even what feelings they inspired. These Amerindian groups had lived in the area for approximately twelve hundred years, but one hundred years after the Europeans arrived, they left in a mass migration at the end of the sixteenth century. The reasons for this are not very clear, but it would be easy to assume that the European interference in their life, the violence of the enslavement, and the constant wars against the invaders were behind their action.

AMERINDIAN FOOD

Cassava (*Manihot esculenta* Crantz), was the main produce of the Tupinambás. Also called *mandioca*, manioc, *aipim*, and yucca, it is a small bush around 1.2 meters tall (4 feet) and has large, oblong dark green leaves; its dark brown roots are its main product. The roots have to be cooked before they are consumed, as they contain cyanide, a poison that evaporates in contact with a heat source. The amount of cyanide varies according to the type of plant.

The roots have a high amount of starch, which allowed a large number of uses in the Amerindian kitchen according to the descriptions by the first visitors to arrive in the Bay of Guanabara. It was used to make flour, which they loved eating plain or with a piece of grilled meat. The flour could also be cooked into a soup with beans or with the plant's leaves, or made into a light porridge they called *mingau*. The name remains in Portuguese. The flour was prepared by peeling, grating, and washing the root; pressing away all the water; and drying the cassava mass in a ceramic plaque over the fire.

The cassava roots could also be fermented into an alcoholic beverage, *Cauim*, which is still prepared today by some Amerindian groups in northern Brazil in the same way the Tupinambás did it in the sixteenth century; therefore, it is possible to reconstruct the recipe. The beverage was prepared by the young women of the group, according to the contemporary testimony of Jean de Léry. They would peel and slice the cassava roots; cook them in water; and then pick small bits out, chew them, and spit them into another vessel. *Cauim* can also be prepared with corn, or with fruits like cashews or pineapples. The cooked mass was chewed in order to break down the sugars in the roots, allowing the cassava mass to ferment, just as grapes were trampled in traditional wine making. The resulting brew was boiled once more and left to ferment and rest like beer.

Flour preparation produced another product, tapioca, which is the residual starch that remains in the vats after the roots are washed in order to make flour. It is a very fine, highly glutinous powder that makes a chewy pancake, also called tapioca.

There were a certain number of fruits gathered in different seasons, such as *pacova*, a type of native banana that has to be grilled or cooked to be consumed. Corn, too, was planted, and the corncob was grilled an eaten as an appetizer. The cooked kernels were also used to prepare fermented drinks.

Salt was acquired by letting seawater dry in ditches, but instead of seasoning ingredients before or while cooking them, they would put a small piece of the cooked food in the mouth and then a little salt, just for the taste of it.

Cassava roots for sale in Rio de Janeiro. *Source*: Marcia Zoladz.

The Tupinambás are an extinct group today; however, they left archaeological traces along the Brazilian coast, including their language, the old Tupi. More important, there were many eyewitness accounts of their culture. They had early contact with the Portuguese, and for a while very close relations with a group of Frenchmen who lived in the Bay of Guanabara; two of whom, Jean de Léry and André Thévet, wrote about their experiences with them. There are similar reports about Amerindian lives in other provinces along the coast that are similar to the Tupinambás in Rio, especially when describing food habits. For ten years, from 1555 to 1565, they exchanged merchandises with the French, mostly brazilwood, which was used to prepare a red dye, and parrots and small monkeys that were sold as pets in Europe.

The Tupinambás were a sedentary people, with a comprehensive knowledge of their land. They used their botanical knowledge to make medicines against fevers and dysentery. They painted their bodies with stains prepared with the fruit of genipapo (*Genipa Americana*) and urucu (*Bixa orellana*). The stains were used in their festivities. Agriculture was the women's work; foraging obeyed a calendar as much as the harvesting of corn, manioc, or the hearts of palms. As for meat, they ate small animals, birds, and fish without opening them, prepared at the moquem, well done, until their skins were scorched.

A typical dish of Rio is tapioca; the cassava starch slightly wet, is sifted, and then heated, the result in a light chewy pancake. *Source*: Marcia Zoladz.

MOQUÉM, THE LOCAL BARBECUE

One of the cooking methods of the local Amerindians was the moquém, the technique used to dehydrate and smoke meats or vegetables. Two or more wood forks supported a grill at a certain distance from the ground over fire embers, thus avoiding the possibility of burning the food and especially the skins of small animals and fish; a large plantain leaf was used to lay mussels over the grill.

Larger animals were cooked wrapped in plantain or palm leaves in order to keep their juices in; smaller ones were cooked with their entrails. They hunted and ate cavies, alligators, armadillos, turtles, and a variety of fish typical of the South Atlantic. Sardines, shrimp, and many small edible fish were grilled in large quantities to feed several groups of families more efficiently.

The best illustrations of the moquém, are ones that show anthropophagic rituals, which were a cause for great discomfort when shown back in Europe. However, once the distaste for looking at an image of arms and legs on the grill has passed, it is easy to relate to the cooking methods.

Larger pieces of meat, according to drawings from the second half of the sixteenth century, were roasted on a skewer staked in the soil close to the fire.

Small animals or fish were grilled on a skewer supported by two forks, all made of wood. When cooking large amounts of food a large grid supported by four stakes would be positioned over the fire, where mussels, shrimps, and small fish covered with pacova leaves would be scattered and cooked. This cooking method allowed the food to dehydrate and therefore was also used for different kinds of meat as a conservation method. The meat, slightly drier, was mixed with cassava flour and easily transported during wartime.

They had a profound knowledge of the fruits of the Atlantic Forest. The *pitanga*, Brazilian cherry (*Eugenia uniflora L.*), is a small red fruit typical of the coast with acid content and a strong aroma, rich in vitamin C. In the same region, there was the native *jabuticaba*, fruit from Brazilian grape tree (*Myrciaria cauliflora*); their trunks bear very sweet black fruits the size of grapes. Close to the rivers there were Ingá (*Inga vera*) with fruits whose seeds were inedible but the pulp around them was good tasting and effective against coughs. Along the coast, trees grew in the sand—*cajus* (*Annacardium occidentale L.*), cashews. The pear-shaped fruits have tannin when not very ripe, and high amounts of vitamin C; the cashew nuts hang from the fruits. Also on the list are *maracujá* (*Passiflora edulis Sims*), passion fruit, a climber later named for its calming qualities; and goiaba (*Psidium guajava L.*), guavas, very aromatic, with their very soft pulp either white or red tinted, the size of small apples, green or light yellow skin when ripe, also rich in vitamin C.

They also collected hearts of palm—*palmito-juçara* (*Euterpe edulis*), and baked them. The heart of the palm is the soft interior of the trunk of more than one type of palm tree; however, not all of them are edible or even soft. The more commonly used species in the Atlantic Forest is the *juçara*, because of its softness and taste in the softer part of the trunk. They baked the trunk in the embers, sliced it open, and ate the interior. Salt and sugar were not part of their diet; rather, they used tiny red and very hot peppers (*Capsicum*) to season their food.

THE PORTUGUESE

When the Portuguese arrived to establish a village, their first intention was to expel French invaders from their land. It was more of a strategic stop on their way to their main commercial interest in India, from where they brought black pepper, cinnamon, cloves, and textiles. This first group, although arriving from the same land, and quite a few being invested as colonial authorities, were composed of a varied group—including sailors, troops, convicts, and new Christians escaping the Inquisition. A heterogeneous group with very few women, they only started to arrive in the seventeenth century. Despite the differences in the diets of these groups while traveling in the ships, being kept in prisons, and living in barracks, the character of the food in Rio started quite soon to take shape. First of all, this was due to a complete lack of other possibilities during a very rigid colonization that closed the harbor to any other nation. Eventually an English fleet could stop for food and water, but could not disembark; therefore, there was time to develop a certain number of local dishes and food habits without an outside influence.

The Portuguese documents telling about life in early colonial Brazil only started to be known to a larger public toward the end of the eighteenth century. The everyday communications from the colony to its capital were the internal affairs of the Portuguese Crown or belonged to religious orders, so they stayed at archives until the nineteenth century, when historians started to study and evaluate them. Printed much later than French and German travel books, these books showed a very precise and accurate assessment of the living conditions. The new inhabitants began to write about their own experiences with sharp eyes, telling what was needed in order to establish a business in Rio. Sometimes a curious note would appear in the text making a picture of everyday life emerge in an especial manner.

By the 1580s, the Catholic Church, in order to prevent enslavement and to reduce local violence, began to protect and group the Amerindian population in enclosures. This intervention led the Portuguese to another solution, already in use in their holdings in North Africa. They brought slaves to Brazil.

EARLY TIMES IN THE BAY OF GUANABARA

The Portuguese took a little longer to colonize the land around Rio de Janeiro, as they were gaining immense profits with the spice trade, especially with black pepper, in the East Indies. Known as early as 1502, the bay was thought at first to be the estuary of a river during a January reconnaissance expedition, hence the name Rio de Janeiro—January River. At first, because it was not very easy to access the bay's small entrance in bad weather the authorities chose a harbor farther south, where the Port of Santos is today. Adding to the natural difficulties, the climate and terrain to the northeast were similar to the possessions of the Portuguese in the Atlantic islands; therefore, colonization began with the same business model of sugarcane plantations and sugar mills in that region. Rio farther south could wait.

They were not alone in these American exploratory expeditions. During these first years—from 1510 to 1550, when the Portuguese colonial occupation was still growing at a slow pace, French merchants interested in establishing more trading posts in the New World built wood-collecting stations along the coast. They also took monkeys, parrots, and other exotic animals to France with them. In this way, the French contributed significantly to the idea that an earthly Paradise could be found in Brazil.

Everything about America was new, the food, the plants, the animals. There were so many contradictory opinions and stories crossing the Atlantic, including mythical tales of golden cities and Amazons on tall horses, that it took almost a century—in some cases even more—to build an accurate portrait of the New World. On one side were the expedition leaders, and Columbus was one of the very first to do this, telling their royal funders that the investment was sound and trying to gain the support of the Church.

An important voice at this time was Pero Vaz de Caminha, the scribe of the first official expedition to Brazil in 1500. After a stop of a few days in Bahia, on their way to India, he ended his first letter to the king of Portugal explaining how the investment would be worthwhile because of the extensive lands, the abundance of good water, and soil as fertile as in the Douro region, the wheat-growing region in Portugal. Moreover, he said the local inhabitants seemed quite docile (their anthropophagic habits were not yet known). He also remembered, rather wisely, to add they would be able to save many souls.

Another source of information was André Thévet's book, *Les singularitez de la France Antartique* (1557), published in France after his stay in the French colony in Guanabara Bay. It greatly fascinated the public with its images of animals, trees, and anthropophagic rituals. These rituals were described with a full understanding of their mythic value, but with detailed explanations of the reasons why not all captured enemies were eaten, only those considered worthwhile.

Christopher Columbus arrived in the New World just after the recapture of Spanish territories from the Moors, an occupation that had begun eight hundred years before. For the past century, the Inquisition had been enlarging its power as more Moorish territories were Christianized. The Catholic Church had a very strong hold over the Spanish Crown, as it did in Portugal; however, certain demands of the inquisitors in Spain—especially the expropriation and the expulsion of the Jews, were attenuated in Portugal, where the Crown offered a second chance for the newly and forcefully converted. For a very high price they could emigrate to the colonies.

The encounter with local populations in Spanish and Portuguese America renewed the opportunities for the Catholic Church to expand its influence. But news of the existence of another continent was filtered through a mixture of political and commercial ideas as well as religious ones. The discovery and exploration of lands previously unknown helped to expand and secularize a concept that until then belonged only to the religious world—Paradise.

A PARADISE?

The idea that Paradise could occupy a real place on Earth took shape at the end of the Middle Ages, and it became even more plausible to a lay audience during the Renaissance when a shift in the theological rhetoric broadened the theme to secularized audiences. The broad concept was that there was a Paradise hidden here on Earth, although it was extremely difficult to reach. This idea of an almost unreachable place acted as an encouragement for those arriving in the New World, as it allowed the search for individual possibilities. Thus Spanish and Portuguese America was a place where an individual could rewrite his personal history freed from European social structures, albeit under the watchful observance of the Catholic Church.

Discussion about the existence of a Paradise on Earth was simultaneous with rising scientific research methods that accompanied the first maritime expeditions. This Paradise, located in the newly discovered continent, was more a part of the material world than of the religious one. Its meaning included the attainment of a wonderful perfect life on Earth, with instant riches.

Greed turned out to be a good companion, for a myth developed around the quest for El Dorado, quite often understood as Paradise on Earth, and soon there were many notices from America of cities completely covered in gold and precious stones. Usually located in the Amazonian and Central American jungles or at the top of very steep mountains, these cities were to be reached only through personal sacrifice. Tales of their existence arrived especially from Mexico and Peru, where the Aztecs and Incas had been exploring mines and making artifacts with gold for centuries. As it happens in most cases, those searching for El Dorado were disappointed. Riches in colonial times were for Crown and Church to acquire, and provincial governments established to explore business opportunities and to convert the natives to Christianity were soon also generating a large amount of riches.

Portuguese America did not have the same symbolic interest in the search for the El Dorado as did Spain, and the Crown did not make the same financial investments in such a search. The Portuguese colonial order was less engaged in developing a mythology and more focused on economically lucrative endeavors. Commentaries by newly arrived bureaucrats and military leaders were mostly down to earth, with descriptions of the qualities of the place and the difficulties of harboring off the coast in order to provision their fleets on their way to India. The Portuguese experience in North Africa, the Azores, and Madeira led to a detachment from the idea of a mythical Paradise. Their initial business model was already well known, with the main agricultural investment in sugarcane plantations and sugar mills, and slaves as a workforce.

Captain Pero Lopes de Souza stayed for three months in the Guanabara Bay in 1531. He noted in his diary: "The people of this river are so kind. . . . The water is excellent. . . . We had the opportunity to collect enough food to maintain four hundred men during one year."[2] It is very far from the idea of a countryside with lonely Amerindians and a few Europeans. Also, considering that more than one fleet would stop for supplies at the same time, the site of the future city always had a small crowd living around its bay. There were different Amerindian groups fighting in the area around the Guanabara Bay, too, and the Portuguese and the French were joining in the battles.

Nevertheless, Rio soon acquired in Europe the image of a paradise; the reasons listed in the first documents are in a certain way quite disappointing when compared to the spectacular mythic quests of the Spanish. The climate, the food, the local population, the healthiness of the place, and the apparent longevity of the locals were important themes. First travelers thought Amerindians could live as long as one hundred and twenty years, perhaps influenced by rumors from Spanish America about the existence of a fountain of youth situated vaguely in the Americas.

In Rio, it was not gold that made the city's fame; rather, it was its geographical location, although a few charming extras did help build this idea of an earthly paradise. First, there was the undeniable impact of the Atlantic Forest in a secluded but very large bay; two large mountains, one of them the Sugar Loaf, half closing its entrance; and the grandiosity of the landscape, which even today is enthralling.

As the ships harbored in the bay, local inhabitants would at first come over and bring food; the longer the Europeans stayed, the more at ease everyone was and the better understood the local customs of the Amerindians. Arrivals at unknown places were not an uncommon situation for these first sailors; after all they had been at sea for some time. They had been to the Portuguese possessions in Africa and in India, stopping in quite a few new lands. They also had been exploring the Brazilian coast and trading with the different local native populations—exchanging animals and natural resources for clothes, tools, and trinkets since early in the sixteenth century.

THE DIFFICULTIES OF EATING IN A FOREIGN LAND

The diversity among the first European inhabitants of the Guanabara Bay helps to build an early picture of Rio de Janeiro. There are the Portuguese first impressions and those of the French, from the city of Rouen, who, despite their short stay—their colony lasted ten years from 1555 to 1565—were already there before in an unofficial way, negotiating fine woods. They were the first to establish the international acknowledgment of the land.

The first step toward understanding the local food implied adopting the ingredients of the local inhabitants. Moreover, the Europeans would have to understand the local agricultural and foraging rhythms. They had arrived in a completely different climate, and needed to learn which animals they should hunt; the different fish species, some of which were poisonous; and all the small decisions of everyday life. It was also necessary to decide how far they were going to adapt themselves to the land and transform their original habits and sometimes their profound religious beliefs in order to survive, as quite a few were not going back to Europe. Not all of the first arrivals were sailors or merchants; there were convicts evicted from Portugal.

Europeans in the Americas had to add new ingredients to their diet to avoid starvation and needed to acquire knowledge about them from their contact with the local inhabitants. Quite a few of these travelers had been in Africa and in India and had a keen eye for new agricultural possibilities, and their travels were part of the business of scouting new opportunities in the New World for their patrons. But part of the Renaissance experience was their individual attraction to a new land so different and distant from their home.

The everyday reality of the living conditions in a colony was very hard, but the richness of the ingredients offered to the new residents resulted in the development of an amazingly large number of new dishes. The main product of the first colonial cycle was sugar, which, combined with the main product of the Amerindian diet, the cassava root and its byproducts, produced an enchanting array of desserts.

The Portuguese dessert recipes prepared in Europe were soon enriched with sweet cakes and puddings made with corn flour, cassava flour, and tapioca, the starch extracted from the cassava root. The local ingredients already in the Amerindian diet when Europeans arrived were soon mixed with eggs, milk, and peanuts instead of almonds, and frequently were covered with a dense caramel sauce. These extremely unctuous sweets were the first to be made in Brazil, where wheat flour was a luxury and remained unavailable for a long time.

Eggs, on the other hand, were readily available, from not only hens and ducks brought by the colonizers but also from local birds and turtles. As the Portuguese already had a traditional sweets repertoire rich in eggs, the development of new desserts was a logical consequence. The traditional Portuguese-Brazilian sweets are an adaptation of the original recipes to local ingredients; it started late in the sixteenth century when nunneries were established in the city and the first European women arrived. The large number of cakes and sweets only got richer as the crossing of the Atlantic became more regular by the late seventeenth century, allowing the constant arrival of all kinds of nuts, raisins, and wines as the elegant dessert lists in menus and the recommendations of sweets and *viennoiseries* found in old notebooks, usually of European origin, attest.

The easy access to sugar in farms and monasteries transformed it from an export commodity into an important fruit preserver. There were two sorts of elegant fruit comfits; in one of them the whole fruit is cooked in sugar syrup for one or more days. In the other, pureed fruits were cooked until malleable enough to be delicately worked into the shape of roses and left to dry in the sun. Most used are the purple sweet potato, quinces, and pumpkin. There are preserves in simple sugar, green papaya, green peaches, and green figs. The several recipes vary according to the fruit and the season. Sugar means good things and abundance in the local culture, and as if a leftover memory from its start as a medicine, it is a custom to serve a little sugar mixed with water for children after a fall or for adults after receiving traumatic news.

Since colonial times the Portuguese developed a unique tradition as businessmen in Rio de Janeiro, importing goods—olive oil, dried codfish, wines—and opening restaurants and dominating the food and drink industry.

SLAVE LIFE AND FOOD IN RIO DE JANEIRO, 1580–1888

The third influence in the food preferences of the inhabitants of Rio came from the involuntary arrivals from Africa, as they were mostly from today's Gulf of Benin, Nigeria, and Sierra Leone, and from the kingdoms of Central Africa and farther south from Angola, Guinea, and Mozambique. The great majority arrived to work in the sugarcane plantations and sugar mills and the tobacco and cotton plantations, and for a short while, they taught the Portuguese how to produce indigo pigment from a native indigo plant in Rio de Janeiro. In the second half of the eighteenth century, when huge deposits of gold and diamonds were discovered in the province of Minas Gerais, Rio was the central arrival port for an ever-increasing number of African slaves.

They arrived to work in the mines and in the city, as it was the official export center of the colony. There they worked as household employees or provided services for the population. They did all sorts of jobs, usually the ones maintained by guilds or associations in Europe—shoe makers, pharmacists, bakers, cooks. They were present in really all areas allowed by the Crown—the city did not have a printing press or large-scale factories or colleges until 1808.

They are the main body of contributors to Rio de Janeiro's cultural ethos in food, in music, and in family relations. They introduced a rich vocabulary, always accompanied by an expressive body language that is so very recognizable as typical of Rio's inhabitants. They speak with diminutive affectionate forms, touch each other with a closer body language, offer food all the time, and keep their groups informed. Information was and still is an important part of the social life in the different groups in Rio.

African influence in the local culture established important patterns of relationships among the city population. The Brazilian fraternal relationships have an African origin, quite a few of them resulting from the systematic destruction of kinship links by slavery—families would be separated after their arrival in Brazil. Therefore, the rebuilt family network is a maze based on affections and religious habits that endure, and in fact flourish, until today. One will choose a brother or sister who is as close as natural kinship, sometimes even more so, as it is a choice.

This fraternal relationship system was also a strong communication network that allowed a local identity, new and distant from the original, to be constructed. Still, many cultural traits of the Cariocas are seen in their habits of singing together, of informing of their whereabouts all the time, almost as a defense technique, of sharing food, of intertwining several religious creeds in a completely original culture.

Religion was and is a part of this identity in the city; the original animistic African rituals that were common to many groups had to be reorganized in the long run. Sometimes groups of the same region would arrive in the city but only after a gap of years. Intermarriage also interfered as much as geographical distances. They kept their original spiritual practices, usually hidden behind Catholic saints, as these *orixás*, or spirits, have very human qualities, and they like to eat. They have to be pleased, and pampered in order to help people keep peace with themselves.

The Candomblé religion in Bahia kept its close ties with Africa, as there was a constant commerce from one continent to the other. And in the 1960s there was a search for its origins. But many of the local religions were based on combinations of several groups with different regional religious experiences. In Rio, the Africans took influences from several religions, including Catholicism and Amerindian beliefs, resulting in a different ritual from that of Candomblé. But in both there is a closeness with the orixás related to food. House altars always have their images with one or two plates of food as an offering in front of them. This structuring period in African-Brazilian religions took many centuries, as the *batuque*, the music played with drums during the ceremonies, was forbidden by the authorities as an independent expression of their culture and religions.

As the large number of different ethnic groups continued to live together, they developed a common language, but even more, they created a new culture, as many arrived as young children. It was a common sight to see young boys of five to ten years for sale at the slave market at the Valongo Pier. According to Mary C. Karasch's book *Slave Life in Rio de Janeiro*[3] 85 percent of the newly arrived were from fifteen to twenty-four years old. As time went by, they were allowed to associate in church brotherhoods to help those in need, to build churches, and to buy their freedom and that of other slaves.

The relationship of slave owners with their slaves was very violent, even when there was not physical punishment. Listed as items of a household in inventories or as objects allowed to be sold in secondhand shops together with chairs or lamps, their lives depended on their ability to work and adapt to the new city. Despite the difficulties, they built a society in a city that developed its cultural vocabulary strongly based and identified with the richness of their contribution.

A mutual influence on both sides of the Atlantic continued during approximately two hundred years, until 1889. With the Republic, the communication between the two continents slowed down. But before that, it was very strong, as the Portuguese understood the facing continents and the Atlantic Ocean in between as one area of its influence. Relations with Spanish-speaking America were more on a political and diplomatic level with smaller cultural exchanges, especially in Rio.

Thus, a Brazilian food ingredient would be exported to Africa and then come back to Brazil as a new dish. It happened with the peppers of the *Capsicum* family, transformed in pepper sauces mixed with palm oil (*Elaeis guineensis*), used in traditional dishes from Bahia, or the natural red food coloring anatto, also called *urucum* (*bixa orellana*), used in fish or chicken dishes but originally a body paint of the Amerindian.

The African contribution to the food of the city has had as many stages as new waves of immigrants. Moreover, they kept arriving from Africa and from internal migrations from other states, a result of economic changes, especially from Bahia, where the sugar cane business was declining. These persons might be African or Brazilians, as the slaves born in the country were called. Therefore, it is very difficult to separate a single specific influence in the food of Rio as strictly African unless there is a witness, as happened with the painter Jean-Baptiste Debret (1768–1848), a Frenchman who lived and traveled extensively in the areas around the city from 1816 to 1831.

In his book *Voyage pittoresque et historique au Brésil*, published when he returned to France, he comments how the food in Rio became more colorful with the arrival from Bahia of slaves of Hausa origin and of Guinean groups. Until then, the Portuguese palate had been the stronger influence in local food, with a parsimonious use of seasonings such as coriander, peppers, and a little turmeric (*Curcuma longa*). Food consisted of vegetables, broths, and cooked meats, mostly pork, but with them also arrived coconut milk—introduced in the province of Pernambuco, in northeast Brazil, by the Dutch while they had a colony in Recife from 1630 to 1654.

Because of an intense commercial interchange from Brazil and Angola, there are many similar dishes on both sides of the Atlantic. One of them is the *moqueca*—a fish stew with tomatoes and red peppers, seasoned with basil, onions, and palm oil. There is also *pirão*, usually served together with fish dishes, not only fish stews. A simple broth is prepared with the head of a fish, a carrot, an onion, some parsley sprigs, and spring onions; at the end a little manioc flour is added to form a cream, it can be thicker or thinner according to taste. Not much, but when served with the seasoned fish it ensures a well-balanced mix. There is also on both sides of the Atlantic the *angu*, the cooked mass of corn flour, not cornstarch, yellow, mellow, and a perfect accompaniment to stews prepared mostly with offal. The cream, also made with manioc, is called *foufou* in West African countries. Angu especially made a name as a street food in a city where most inhabitants were young men, either slaves, freemen, sailors, students, or clerks, who needed to have a hearty meal.

HOW TO PREPARE ANGU DE QUITANDEIRA, OR THE EARLIEST POPULAR STREET FOOD

This is one of the oldest dishes sold in the streets of the city. It is a corn flour porridge served together with a dense, slow-cooked mix of offal—heart; kidney; liver; ox tail; and pieces of beef, lamb, or pork, the result is a hearty and tasty stew. Angu is the corn flour stew and *quitandeira* is a word that means women who sold good food or vegetables. African women had a monopoly as quitandeiras in colonial and imperial Brazil; they would assemble in large stands with their cauldrons in a square or close by a fountain, and soon a variety of patrons would buy their food. The cooking and the movement around the food stalls became a favorite subject among foreign painters visiting the city in the early nineteenth century. Their watercolors usually depict three or four women in charge of their cauldrons surrounded by a small crowd.

Angu made with a varying assortment of offal meats is almost a lost tradition, but as the following recipe from a 1906 notebook attests, it was a welcome dish in elite and middle-class homes at the time. A rich, slow-cooked stew with plenty of subtle flavors, it may have been continuously prepared in the same pot with more water, meat, and seasonings added every day, hence its reputation as unhealthy and filthy food. It probably had—and this is an exercise in imagination—a well-caramelized taste.

Considered a poor man's fare, in addition to the street vendors it was sold in the *zungus*, the first popular eateries in the city. *Zungu* is a Brazilian adaptation of *nzangu*, which means "noise" in Kimbundu, a language spoken in today's Angola. Another interpretation for the word is "the house where angu is sold." It was a place where slaves and freedmen gathered to drink and eat; usually they lived in the same building.

The dish, or rather its milieu, was considered a public health menace, criticized, like many other such dishes and the places where they were sold, as a source of sickness. Nevertheless, it survived, and today one can still eat it downtown were the old harbor used to be in the nineteenth century at the restaurant Angu do Gomes. It can be prepared in a lighter version with stewed tongue, but then it is not the Angu de Quitandeira!

To prepare it, cut into small pieces any portion of liver, heart, tongue, or other variety of meat and cook in salted water. The next day, make a stew with all the seasonings—lime juice, onions, tomatoes, chilies, and red peppers—and lard. After it is ready, sprinkle with parsley and add a little palm oil. In a separate pan make the Angu, either with corn flour with a little cassava flour or with rice flour. Add three or four small chili peppers.

RECIPE FOR MOQUECA DE CAMARÃO, A FESTIVE SEAFOOD DISH

This recipe has its origins in the Afro-Brazilian kitchen. Today it is part of the Carioca festive repertoire, usually one single dish of African origin with several complements such as salads. However, this recipe is from a family

Angu sellers on the streets of Rio de Janeiro. *Source*: Engraving by Jean-Baptiste Debret, *Voyages Pictoresque au Brésil*, 1826, http://www.brasiliana.usp.br/bbd/handle/1918/00624520.

notebook from 1906. At that time it was served as a fish or shrimp stew, probably on the same day that they were bought. Moqueca is very easy to prepare, so each household developed its own special seasoning, and it can be prepared either with a mixed variety of fish, crabs, and other seafood or with one of them alone. It is also in the list of recipes defined as *à baiana*—dishes with origins in the northeastern state of Bahia or ones that use palm oil as an ingredient.

Start by washing, peeling, and deveining the shrimps, keeping the heads attached. Season them with salt, lemon juice, and a little bit of chili peppers and let them rest until right before cooking. In a large pan, arrange the shrimps in enough oil and, if desired, a little oil of palm; top with a few sliced tomatoes, onions, parsley, and chives.

Cover the pan and cook for ten to fifteen minutes in very high heat on the stovetop. Serve with angu prepared with corn flour or rice flour. The latter, also called *acaçá*, has all but disappeared from Rio's tables.

A SMALL GLOSSARY OF THINGS
EVERYBODY KNOWS IN RIO

à baiana: Prepared in the manner of or with ingredients typical of foods in Bahia, a state in northeast Brazil. Usually with African roots, a large majority are prepared with seafood, aromatic herbs, and onions, sometimes with okra or tomatoes. Palm oil with its characteristic taste and red peppers are also common ingredients in the recipes.

limão: The yellow fruit called lemon in English (*Citrus limon*) is known as *limão-Siciliano* (Sicilian lemon) in Brazil, whereas, all types of limes are also called *limão* (lemon) in Portuguese. There are three types of limes commonly used in cakes, alcoholic drinks, and lemonades:

1. *limão-taiti* (*Citrus* x *latifolia*)—large or medium-size green limes with a thin or uneven skin, very acidic;
2. *limão-galego* (*Citrus aurantifolia*), tiny, light green, with a higher sugar content, and
3. *limão-rosa* (rose lemon) also called *limão-cravo* (clove lemon) (*Citrus* x *limonia*), when unripe it has a green skin; the shape is similar to a tangerine when ripe, and its pulp is always orange colored, the less acidic of the three.

moqueca: Stew, mostly used in reference to fish and seafood dishes that use palm oil in its ingredients. The word is a variation of *mukeka*, one of the different African languages spoken in colonial times. It is prepared in a shallow, large-mouthed ceramic pot.

oleo de dendê: Palm oil (*Elaeis guineensis*) is the oil obtained by pressing its fruit. It is an East African plant introduced in Brazil in the seventeenth century. It is used in recipes from Bahia.

quitandeira: A woman who sells fruits and vegetables, sometimes cakes, hot puddings, and doughnuts. The name originates in the word *quitanda*, the articles sold by these women, especially sweets and delicate biscuits. They also sold their food on large wooden boards called *tabuleiros* around the city, and the recipe got its ancient name from them.

THE FRENCH IN BRAZIL

There has been a fascination with the French in the local culture and geography of Rio de Janeiro since they first arrived in the Bay of Guanabara, and the city inhabitants developed a long-term reciprocity. At first, they were mostly Normans from northern France, searching for *Pau-Brasil* (*Caesalpinia echinata*), brazilwood, on the Brazilian coast. The tree was highly valuable since its wood served to make a red pigment with a tint of orange used in the textile industry.

Red pigment had several hues and different sources, all highly valued. Real red pigment, obtained at the time from the dried kermes insect, resulted in crimson red. The vivid red pigment was a highly poisonous stain that intoxicated painters and dyers as it was obtained by burning white lead until achieving the desired hue. During the Renaissance a new red ink was introduced in Europe, obtained by crushing the cochineal, an insect from Mexico. Its vivid red, seen in Aztec and Inca clothes, had enchanted the Spanish invaders, who enlarged its production and exported it.

The French had a presence in the city's culture throughout the centuries. Curiously, their participation was at first important in a material sense—as independent brazilwood buyers and as explorers with a colony on an island in the Guanabara Bay, the *France Antarctique*, from 1555 to 1565. They also sent the first parrots and small monkeys to France. In 1710 and 1712, Rio suffered two corsair attacks that, with the cannonade and plundering, added much to the image of the French as intrepid.

Today they comprise the largest number of foreign students in Brazilian universities, and over the centuries the French have had a large influence in intellectual circles in Brazil. Already in the eighteenth century their ideas of freedom were brought to the country; their books were secretly read, and in response to excessive taxes, stimulated a revolt against the Portuguese Crown in 1789. The revolt started in the mining region of Minas Gerais, and as expected, the rebels were betrayed. Their trial, held in Rio for greater impact, resulted in the hanging of their leader, called Tiradentes. The other insurgents were either exiled to Angola, then a Portuguese possession, or sentenced to prison.

The main inspiration for the rebellion was the American Revolution of 1776, and the reason for the Crown's suppression of it was an endemic fear that the idea of a democracy in the United States, the industrial revolution in England, and the liberal ideas from France would spread through the country. Among the inspirational books found with the rebels was a French translation of the American Constitution originally published in 1776.[4] Another important book was the *Encyclopédie ou dictionnaire raisonné des sciences, des arts et des métiers*, published by Diderot and D'Alembert in 1751, and at the time it was as prohibited in France as in Brazil.

A public school system was created in Rio after the arrival of the Portuguese court in 1808, but prior to that there was a small confessional schooling system centered in the convents or in homes with private instructors and governesses, a number of them from France. A collective idea about France and in a similar way a strong desire from the French to be part of the Brazilian life thus developed. It encouraged future generations to develop scientific research together with French universities and research programs that continues to this day.

A French culinary influence started in Brazilian food in the second half of the nineteenth century. Frenchmen opened hotels with good chefs, and with a constant flow of French immigrants arriving to work in commercial companies, their restaurants and catering services soon began to open and flourish. As the capital of an independent empire south of the equator, Rio took France as a model in creating many of its new institutions. The list of dishes at social and business gatherings began to change, which influenced the development of bourgeois cuisine in the large spa towns close to the city and vacation places for rich Brazilians. Access to leisure travel abroad also became more common in the upper classes, which also brought new recipes to the city. Likewise, the French also influenced the image of Brazil in Europe. They were the first to publish a widely known pictorial representation of the country, depicting the land and the city as a place full of adventures and many riches.

THE AMERINDIANS IN FRANCE

As in many colonial cities, Rio built its image on its own cultural strengths, while always looking for foreign acclaim. In the early sixteenth century, there were many Brazilian-themed entertainments in France. They exhibited the exoticism of this New World population and became a frequent way to amuse the inhabitants of a city like Rouen, for instance, where the majority of festivities took place. What could be understood as a very exotic show was in fact a way of sharing more information about a typical commercial exchange in the Guanabara Bay, as evidenced by notices of more than one such staged setting starting from 1527. Thus it made sense for the common people and for the bourgeoisie to invite the Tupinambás to exhibit their lifestyle in France. The result was an image of an exciting place with adventurous opportunities.

Brazil, and the Tupinambá, continued to have an impact on the French imagination as their colonial world expanded. When they started to explore the eastern coast of Canada, for example, they found a plant with an edible root they called *toupinambour*, Jerusalem artichoke, because it reminded them of the root of cassava and of the Brazilian yam, cará (*Dioscorea trifida*).

Starting in 1520 and extending through a period of approximately thirty years, Royal visits and ensuing festivities were quite "the thing" in the life of a French city. The themes staged and the decorative motives used along the way were usually of religious order as the visit's purpose was to ensure the king's power and renew local alliances. In 1850, Ferdinand Denis, a French historian who specialized in the history of Brazil and Portugal, found a three-hundred-year-old pamphlet with plans for a Brazilian Festival, considered the first iconographic document about Brazil in the press in the sixteenth century. It included twenty-nine wood engravings and described in detail King Henry II's entry into the city, the high point of such festivities. The "Figure des Brésilliens," a theatrical portrayal of the combat between two enemy tribes—with real Amerindians brought from Brazil, sailors dressed as Amerindians, monkeys, and parrots—was a small part of the celebrations, but it must indeed have been memorable.

The importation of small animals such as tiny marmoset monkeys, green parrots (the ones that learn to speak), and macaws of the Atlantic Forest brought as gifts to expedition fundraisers and aristocrats stimulated the European imagination. They were an attraction for possible businesses developments with a fixed colony, a fort, a priest, and hopefully the possession of the land nearby. Three books of great success also made Rio de Janeiro and the exotica around it quite well known in Europe. The first book to be published was Franciscan friar André Thévet's *Les singularitez de la France Antarctique*, published in 1557 to great success and fame; the second, written by the Protestant theologian Jean de Léry, was *Histoire d'un voyage fait en la terre du Brésil*. Both men visited the French colony—*France Antarctique*—Antarctic France, around the same time.

The third book, *Zwei Reisen nach Brasilien—1544–1555* (*Two Travels to Brazil*), was written by Hans Staden, a German mercenary who lived among the same Tupinambás, only farther south. According to his text, he escaped twice from being eaten during anthropophagic rituals. He told about his life with the Amerindians to a larger public and described in detail their cannibalism.

All three authors told about life in the same ethnic group; André Thévet arose to great prestige and was assigned the position of cosmographer to the king of France after his book was published. According to Jean de Léry, he did not see much, as he never left the French fortress during his stay; however, he was responsible for introducing a new world to the European imagination. Of the two, one would tend to see in Léry's book a more levelheaded testimony; after all, he was the one who really saw everyday habits among the Amerindians. After returning from Brazil he led an adventurous life during the religious wars in France in the sixteenth century, and his book was not published until much later in 1578.

Thévet and Hans Staden were the first foreign sources to tell about life in the tropics. It is a joy to see their pleasure in telling their adventures living in an exotic and expansive landscape for their readers. Even if from today's point of view their impressions are somewhat embellished or imagined, they represent the impact of the new land on these writers, and its enchantment is undeniable. The books with their rich engravings and the spectacle of the Brazilian Festival introduced a very favorable image of the country in the foreign mind, which endures today.

Rio de Janeiro, more than any other city, embodies well the description of a place that triggers the creative process in many areas: art, food, film, architecture. Every century brought at least one exchange that left a strong cultural trace either in Rio or in France. Just one of many examples is the musical series by Darius Milhaud, *Le boeuf sur le toît*, from 1920. It was inspired in the rhythms of Brazilian popular music, which he learned when he worked in Rio as a secretary at the French Embassy, in 1916–1917. Another is the 1959 film *Orfeu do Carnaval* (*Black Orpheus*), written and directed by Marcel Camus, with music and lyrics by Antonio Carlos Jobim and Vinicius de Moraes, who would delight us later with "The Girl from Ipanema."

There was, and there is, a mutual admiration between France and Brazil that shows itself in the city with constant art exhibits of French artists, conferences, and University exchanges. It is a two-way road, with a large number of Brazilian academics, students, and artists living and researching in France. One of the most successful traits of French culture in Brazil is in the food. It is so deeply ingrained in the local table that the Cariocas do not even notice when they cook using French methods for their sauces or desserts. It is true they are mostly an inheritance of the bourgeois cuisine of the late nineteenth century, but even so, one can buy at street markets or eat at coffeehouses *madeleines*, *financiers*, and *palmiers*, for example, together with their coffee with no translation needed for their names.

Food in Rio is exactly like its population—extremely modern and adherent to its popular culture, food defined by its freshness. The best praise a restaurant can receive is that they serve very good household food. Gourmets and chefs have a hard time in their efforts to captivate their public.

HANS STADEN, A NOTE

At the height of the period of discoveries in the Americas, one of the most shocking was the cannibalism rituals of many Amerindian groups. It was quite an overpowering concept that muted for a while many other important features of tropical culture and the Amerindians with their rich contribution to food and to cooking methods.

One book especially aroused curiosity about the existence of people who ate people under certain circumstances in Brazil. The adventures of Hans Staden, published in Europe in 1557, with the attractive name *True Story and Description of a Country of Wild, Naked, Grim, Man-Eating People in the New World, America*.[5] The book had a series of woodcut illustrations showing in detail what happened to captured Amerindian enemies. Later the woodcuts were replaced with sophisticated engravings in an edition by Theodor de Bry, in Frankfurt, in 1593. His storytelling enthralled the European world, achieving the status of a bestseller with seventy editions in several languages including Latin.

As it happened, at first Staden's reports from the New World were so amazing that many doubted his identity. He was born in Germany, in the city of Homburg, in 1525, and died in Wolfhagen, in 1576. There were more doubts about his luck in escaping twice the Tupinambás. Some speculated that perhaps he had put together a few stories he heard in his travels. There were other reports of cannibalism during the sixteenth century in Brazil.

There were practical discussions about the political status of the original inhabitants of the Americas during the whole colonial period in the Americas, directly related to property concerns of the European governments. These debates included the question of servitude and enslavement of the natives as well as indignant reports concerning their extermination, whether in warfare against the invaders or from disease such as smallpox, which wiped out entire peoples. Already in the early period of the colonization of the New World by the Spanish and Portuguese alike, the Catholic Church, with priests such as the Jesuit Manoel da Nóbrega in Brazil and the Dominican friar Bartolome De Las Casas, were questioning the treatment of the local population.

The impact of the report about cannibalism and the ensuing discussion was an important part of the expansion of the major powers during the sixteenth and seventeenth centuries, but it started a philosophical questioning of the political powers in Europe. Eating a captured enemy after a war was a ritual practice of the Amerindians—as Hans Staden clearly explained in his book—not an everyday feature of their diet. What he could not know was that his account of his adventures would start a long-term philosophical discussion about Amerindian life, but also about freedom and human rights. These discussions sometimes had the intent of understanding a new culture that was showing itself to the Europeans, other times they took on a literary or metaphoric sense, as when Montaigne used cannibalism to write about social inequalities in France.

PORTUGUESE AND AFRICAN, BUT COMPLETELY CARIOCA

The originality of the different dishes of the Rio table is the result of the layering of several influences. At first, regional food was created by amalgamating the available ingredients, the ones introduced by the Europeans, and imported ones. Without the ingredients of their original dishes, Europeans and African had to acquire the local food ways. Everybody that lived in Rio in its first three hundred years—that is, during its colonial period—was outside the comfort zone of his or her own culture. The Amerindians of the Termininós and Tupinambás groups had to share their traditions while at the same time accommodating the tastes and new ingredients of the first Europeans. Many of the colonists also had to learn how to cook in a Christian way, since most of them, either as representatives of a capital venture or the investors themselves, were Jews converted to Christianity in order to escape from Europe, and they were under the scrutiny and pressure of the Church's Inquisition. Common thieves and political enemies also arrived, having been given exile sentences in order to enlarge the number of men in the new colonies. These belonged to the lower classes in Portugal—sailors, farmers, or city workers—and not all had the necessary skills to explore a new land and feed themselves. And finally, Africans were arriving from two different latitudes. They came from the ports of Cabinda and Luanda and from the northwestern African coast, from the region of the Bight of Benin, the coast of Senegal, and Cameroon. With them came even more new religious and cultural contributions, including Islam.

In order to understand how the African presence was important in the construction of the cultural life of the city of Rio de Janeiro it is important to realize that these people belonged to a number of different ethnic groups. According to historian Alberto Costa e Silva,[6] they were not only from the Yoruba, one of the largest ethnic groups of today's Ghana and Mali, but also Fon, from Benin and southern Ghana, and Hausa from Sudan and the Sahel regions. There were people from the Kanen-Bornu kingdom, located between Libya and Chad on a rich caravan road they controlled; Nupe from Nigeria; Fante from today's southern Ghana; and so many others with distinct cultures and life experiences. A diverse group that included herders, cattle breeders, goldsmiths, dyers, farmers, and many others, they all brought a variety of foodways that were absorbed by the local population.

It is impossible to separate the African influence from the food and the life of the inhabitants of the city; it is also impossible to establish one single African culture. As the colonial enterprise grew, so did the number of slaves. As many as 4.9 million African men, women, and children arrived in Brazil from 1540 until 1850, according to information gathered in the Trans-Atlantic Slave Trade Database,[7] even after the prohibition of the transport of slaves across the Atlantic Ocean. Most arrived in the harbor of the city especially after the first half of the eighteenth century.

In addition to these people, who did not always speak the same language, there were large numbers of Brazilians of African origin born in the country, who spoke Portuguese, as well as internal migrants from various linguistic groups who moved to Rio for any number of reasons, such as herding cattle to be sold and then staying on. There were also migrants from economically distressed areas and those expelled for causing political upheavals, and these arrived with their own regional ingredients and eating and cooking habits.

Understanding the intertwined dependence of slaves and their owners for a formal existence in the city helps to explain why and how Africans and the Brazilian black community had such an important positive contribution to life in Rio. There were slaves who had slaves; there were slaves who had their own orchards and sold their crops at the city markets, sharing the profits with their owners; there were freedmen who bought slaves to work for them.

The Portuguese, being interested only in the commercial side of the colonial enterprise, created no local institutions except ones related to the enrichment of the Crown. They established a police department, a tax collecting system, a slave punishment system, a slave market, and Church missions. Not until the early nineteenth century did they establish or fund a college or university. In a way, this institutional abandonment allowed the cultural diversity among the population to settle into a less stratified cultural unification in Rio. The elite had business and family links with Lisbon, but they were in small number compared with all the other nationals.

Not all the plants of Brazil were completely unfamiliar to the newly arrived, but because one tends to describe what is new, it seemed as if they were landing indeed in an unknown world. New agricultural knowledge had to be learned in order to exploit it to economic advantage. Some local plants, like tobacco, would soon develop to the colony's advantage, others to feed the new inhabitants. Cassava was one of these latter plants, a local staple of the Amerindian groups.

Beans were similar to the pulses or chickpeas used in Mediterranean cuisine, so they were planted in the same gardens and farms with the Portuguese grains and vegetables. The Africans who took part in the transatlantic slave trade also imported okra and adapted new species of yams (*Discorea rotundata*) to the native *cará*. Reciprocally, cassava and peanuts were brought back and adapted in Africa and corn spread to Portugal. The Portuguese brought their own crops, cattle, and hens. Rice arrived from Portugal quite early. Some even say that Pedro Álvares Cabral brought seeds in his first expedition to the country in 1500, as it was already consumed in Portugal, but only in 1766 did the Crown authorize the first rice milling facility.

The city became an important market for Portuguese products, from wheat flour to olive oil to cheeses to nuts, as well as scissors, knives, cutlery, kitchenware, and tableware; they all had to be imported since the Crown did not allow the country to develop any industry. Agricultural enterprises were managed with a tight fist, and certain items such as fish, cassava, beans, and fruits were considered foods for slaves. But as their consumption was not restricted, all the local population ate them and included them in their recipes, developing what would later become the favorites of their tables.

Africans arriving to work in Brazil as slaves were not always sent to work in agricultural areas. A large number remained in the city. Rio was the largest harbor in the country, which meant that a vast number of Africans found urban employment, but not necessarily in a house. Slaves were frequently employed as a way to enlarge household earnings, working on the streets of the city for their owners offering a large variety of services such as carrying water and transporting people in sedans or in hammocks. They also worked as journeymen and had to bring home a certain amount of money; the fees for their services were negotiated with their clients allowing a small gain. This money might be saved to buy their freedom or to buy a slave in order to enlarge their businesses.

With the city's multitude of ethnic variations and an almost insurmountable communication maze of so many languages, perhaps food became a way to circumvent the differences; everybody ate cassava roots, quite a few beans, rice, meat—cattle, pork, poultry—and fish in multiple possible dishes. Food in Rio has its origin less in the national identity of the groups arriving in the city than in their religious links. At first there were the Amerindians, soon followed by New Christians and Catholics, then several African peoples with multiple religions and languages.

As the nineteenth century progressed, minorities from the Ottoman Empire, Jews, and Orthodox Christians arrived and went to live in the same areas of the city until then populated by ex-slaves in downtown Rio. This closeness somehow added to a very special intermingled table in a city where rich and poor appreciate the same food values. They took the Portuguese food and mixed it with their knowledge of tropical agriculture; used the local pepper, *capsicum*, in multiple sauces dried or raw; and flavored and colored the food in red with native plants like annatto (*Bixa orellana*). Eventually the city population created its food vocabulary with the variety of preferences and little habits that make local foodways so recognizable in every culture.

Chapter Three

What Is the Food
Legacy of Later Immigration?

There are several ways of understanding the meaning of local food; one of them is from the point of view of the people who have recently arrived in a new place and find it is not very easy to keep the foodways of their families. The circumstances are new, and the meaning of food starts to change. Dishes the cook used to prepare need to be adapted. In a tropical land, the new house has a different architecture, a different kitchen layout, and a different oven. And even if the same flour, or the same herbs are used, grown in another soil and mixed with a different salt, the result is a different dish. The estrangement from the original flavor is also the start of the adaptation process, since food will never taste like grandmother's and the local dishes will have to become part of everyday life.

The richness of the local culture of Rio de Janeiro was introduced in the life of the immigrants at this precise moment of the adaptation process. The list of dishes and cooking methods were renewed at the same time the Portuguese language entered their everyday lives.

In Rio, there is a tendency to cultural dilution in the kitchen. Dilution is a better word than fusion because there is no intentional search for a new repertory of dishes; rather, there is a constant dialogue with the tropical climate and ingredients availability. Bananas will be used in the Austrian Strudel instead of apples; or the kibbeh, the ground beef dish from the Middle East, will be prepared without *za'atar*; or pine nuts, more difficult to obtain, will be replaced with the traditional Portuguese braised onion and garlic mix. This process has repeated itself with dishes from all over the world in the last four hundred years.

Even if the majority of the ingredients were available, immigrants were most of the time too young to know much about cooking methods. They were young men or teenagers, arriving to work in the shops of some relative or friend of the family. The vast majority worked and slept in the same place, quite a few just for room and board.

Single men would rent a room in one of the several boardinghouses serving home food; it was not their original family dishes, but it came to represent what these young foreigners understood as everyday food. This array of dishes was what these young working people ate. There were women too, and they took the boardinghouse menu to their homes when they married. The list of recipes can be seen in contemporary notebooks. Traditional Carioca dishes were already there: green beans soufflés, braised meat with a thick velvety sauce, cauliflower cream soup, and prawns sautéed with chayote.

Here too, an interesting sociocultural phenomenon took place, not so easy to quantify, but experienced in many immigrant families. In order to be accepted by the locals, newcomers used these new dishes to show how they were well adapted to their surroundings. To be a Carioca meant to eat a lunch of rice and black beans with a little manioc flour sprinkled over it and a small steak or a grilled piece of chicken, to drink cold mate, and to have a piece of watermelon for dessert.

The exchange of recipes, and the ensuing cultural interrelation was quite simple. For instance, during the 1930s, two young women living in the same neighborhood, one from Spain and the other from Poland, might talk about what they were cooking for their children. One would say she heard that black beans were very healthy; the other would give her the recipe and add that she should cook some meat with the beans. She would also say someone told her that liver steak should be served once a week. One must remember that inexpensive meat was a novelty for Europeans. A Brazilian neighbor from the northeast of the country living on the other side of the street might explain how to prepare the rice. The children from both neighbors would taste a *cocada*—a coconut and sugar brittle—at the neighbor's house, and the recipe would soon be a loved one for the two European women.

Lunch was easier to prepare than it is today, as the majority of the household members would be at home. Until the 1960s, men would sometimes come home to eat—at least in certain work groups. Workers might eat at the factories and construction workers would carry their own lunch, but doctors and lawyers or civil servants would lunch at home.

Dinner for the elite and the middle classes was a more formal affair; the table settings were more ornate, and it could start with a vegetable soup or a chicken bouillon followed by roasted loin of pork or a grilled fish, always with a sauce, and rice and vegetables. Black beans were not served at dinner, at least for adults. However, vegetables were always present at lunch and dinnertime. There was a certain distinction between the vegetables and the ways they were prepared for lunch and dinner. The ones considered local and more common were and still

Traditional black beans served with cured or dried meats, sprinkled with cassava flour; the orange slices on the side served as a digestive. *Source*: Marcia Zoladz.

are for lunch; they include chayote, *jiló* (*Solanum gilo*), in English called scarlet eggplant, *maxixe* (*Cucumis anguria L.*), from the family of the cucumbers, okra or one or more types of yams, taro, sweet potatoes, and green beans. Well, nothing a béchamel sauce or a gratin could not upgrade. But dinner really favored purées and grilled or baked potatoes, small cheese quiches—*empadinhas*—and rice, the meat, poultry, or fish served together with a sauce.

There used to be a distinction between national ingredients and upgraded, or rather imported, ingredients, such as French green beans or the different kinds of chicory—frisées or endives in their original country—like the elongated Japanese turnip. These were new seeds introduced by a new generation of gardeners, quite a few Japanese families with large orchards in the greenbelt around Rio, and especially in the state of São Paulo. But today the focus is more on the nutritional value of a dish and is based on the amount of different colors one has in a dish—at least four to have the necessary daily supplements—the importance of organic agriculture, and healthy ingredients. The social status somehow left the table, and for a good cause.

The result of the tension between local habits and foreign ones was a new gastronomic identity. A banquet to which all the nations contributed, enriching the meals of the city.

> Um, dois, feijão com arroz
> Três, quarto, feijão no prato
> Cinco, seis, chegou minha vez
> Sete, oito, comer biscoito
> Nove, dez, comer pasteis
>
> One, two, beans with rice
> Three, four, beans in the plate
> Five, six, now it is my turn
> Seven, eight eat cookies
> Nine, ten, eat dumplings

The popular children's rhyme above points to universality of beans and rice as the first real food offered to young children in Brazil. Cariocas grow up with the idea of rice and beans as the traditional home food of the country. Black beans are favored in Rio de Janeiro; different regions throughout the country cook the same dish with different types of beans, their colors varying from light brown to dark brown or black.

The white rice, prepared pilaf style, is the nucleus of the meal, with beans on the side. To these one will add a variety of the traditional dishes immigrants have brought in. At first immigrants might add the rice and beans combination rather timidly into their weekly menus, but soon it was an ingrained habit in all the households in Rio. It is usually at lunchtime meal, as black beans, except when prepared as a soup, are regarded as a heavy dish, therefore unsuitable for dinnertime; a popular myth was that they were prone to give nightmares. There is a lighter version for children only with the *caldinho*, the black broth, without the beans.

Lunchtime reveals the immigration of Western and Central European working-class culture to the city. A single household might prepare in the same week cooked ox tongue served with potato purée prepared in the German way, nicely browned liver steaks served together with braised onions straight from Portugal, and meatballs prepared in the Italian style in very little tomato sauce. Also common are sardines and fried or grilled fish fillets, always served with the rice and beans combination, sometimes with farofa (see below).

All of these dishes are considered home food today, not foreign. As side dishes, green beans, spinach, or cauliflower with a simple béchamel sauce, a cream prepared with corn grains, is also a favorite. A simple salad will be arranged with lettuce, tomato, and onions, all very fresh, with oil and vinegar on the side.

Another way to understand home food is from the angle of where it is served. This type of inexpensive, popular food can be found served for lunch as the *prato feito*, or PF—that is, the low-priced *plat du jour* found at bars and small restaurants (*botequins*) and bakeries.

FAROFA! AN EXPLANATION

One of the most beloved dishes in Rio is farofa. Like many of the foods originating in a colony, farofa resulted from a fusion following a culture clash, in this case between the Amerindians and the Portuguese. By its description it is not a dish one would be very enthusiastic about, as it is not a succulent fare. However, it is really loved by adults and children. Older children love to play a game with younger ones, asking them to try to say "farofa" with their mouth full, usually with comical results.

When the Portuguese arrived, there was no wheat in the land. The Amerindians prepared flour with the roots of cassava. As so often happens when different cultures settle down together, its ingredients were adapted and used according to the availability of local produce and the cultural background of the cook. Farofa is a good example because its origins can be seen as a trimmed-down version of the North African couscous.

Farofa is a well-seasoned mix of manioc flour, eggs, thinly sliced onions rings, green kale finely shredded, and a little bacon cut in tiny pieces. It is a side dish, part of the traditional everyday fare of rice and black beans and served with a steak or a meat stew. There are richer versions with sliced bananas and a vegetarian version without the eggs or bacon. Contemporary versions also add Brazil nuts from the Amazon region or one of the many sophisticated flavors from Central Brazil, such as the nuts from the Baru fruit (*Dipteryx alata*). Manioc flour, just like the semolina used in couscous, is a good flavor carrier and capable of holding moisture in its grains.

If farofa was at first an adaptation of North African couscous, as time went by it became deeply ingrained in the national identity, with plenty of regional variations. More importantly, it was served without the explanations that so often accompany a dish in an ex-colonial land: "Ah! This egg cream we inherited from the Portuguese." As if the European origin would make it better tasting. Or, again, "We learned the *moqueca* from the Africans" —which is true, without them there would be no fish cooked with coconut milk, but it seems ex-colony inhabitants feel anything good has to come from outside of their land to be valued—although the African population created the dish in Brazil, since it needs the native *Capsicum* pepper. But the one exception to such explanations in Rio is the farofa—a genuine native dish served without excuses.

As noted, it was not a completely native dish; it had is origin in couscous, a dish of Berber origin made with semolina steamed in a special pan and served together with a meat or a vegetable stew. It arrived in Portugal during the period of Moorish domination, 711–1249. According to Isabel Maria Fernandes, couscous was served to King João III in 1524,[1] although fifty years later it was probably replaced with some other dish since the steamer needed for cooking the semolina was not mentioned in tax bills regarding the pans manufactured by the potters of Coimbra after 1573. Couscous had probably lost its place in the Portuguese menu to rice from Asia and corn flour, *fubá*, newly arrived from Brazil.

In the sixteenth century, there was no wheat in Brazil, but there were several kinds of manioc/cassava flour. When the first inhabitants established themselves in the city in 1565, couscous was still prepared and sold in the streets of Lisbon; therefore, they were used to eating either rice or semolina with a stew.

In Brazil, *couscous* became the general name for steamed dishes; it means both a savory dish and a sweet cake. The fluffy textured Moroccan dish, prepared with semolina, is available in large supermarket chains in Rio and in São Paulo, and it is one of the exotic ingredients for sale in the country, but this is not the savory Brazilian homemade variety prepared with a mix of cassava and corn flour, also called bread in the northeast. Only the cooking method used to be the same, both were steamed. Today, Moroccan or North Africa couscous comes in packages with the semolina grains already precooked; there is no need to steam the semolina pellets any more.

In Rio, couscous is a sweet dish; it is not a dessert but a snack sold by street vendors and consumed by children after school or at breakfasts and brunches. Prepared with tapioca grains soaked in milk and coconut milk with almost no sugar added, it is covered with shredded coconut and, as a treat, a little (or a lot of) sweet condensed milk drizzled over it. In the past, tapioca grains were steamed until soft to acquire the consistency of a pudding. Today, tapioca couscous is prepared by soaking the grains overnight in milk.

Farofa, interestingly, is the only dish that looks like a Moroccan couscous, it has a similar taste—but it is otherwise prepared directly in a casserole. Onions, garlic, eggs, bananas, or shredded Portuguese green kale braised in pork fat or oil are mixed with cassava flour only at the end. It is never associated with its ancestor.

The ingredients in farofa result in a dish that coincidentally blends the first cultural influences in Brazilian food. A farofa is 100 percent local. The flour is made of cassava and eggs (i.e., of chickens), which arrived with the first settlers in the sixteenth century. Amerindians did not have them, although they did consume the eggs of several birds and turtles. Green kale was transplanted from Portugal, as was all the pork products.

Farofa

Cassava flour mixed with different ingredients makes for the most popular side dish in the city. Besides eggs and green kale, bacon or bananas cut in thick slices can also be added. Sometimes butter or coconut fat is used instead of vegetable oil or the original pork fat.

1 cup green kale leaves (see in the recipe how to prepare them)
1 medium-size onion, minced
1 clove of garlic, minced
3–5 tablespoons corn, soy, or canola oil
2 eggs
½ teaspoon salt
½ teaspoon ground black pepper
3 cups cassava flour

Start by washing the kale leaves, cutting off the hard center stem. Stack them and roll them up tightly, and cut into very thin slices with a large and very sharp knife.

Cook the onion and the garlic in the oil over a low heat until the onions are soft and start to gain color. Add the eggs, scrambling them until almost cooked—they need to keep their moisture. Season with salt and pepper, the amount of salt is very small.

Add the kale, shake the pan to spread its content evenly, and start adding the cassava flour, continuously stirring until all the ingredients are well distributed.

Tapioca Couscous

Traditionally covered only with shredded coconut, today it is drizzled with sweet condensed milk.

1⅔ cups milk
1 cup shredded coconut
1 cup granular tapioca, or quick-cooking
3 tablespoons sugar
¼ teaspoon salt
¼ teaspoon grated lemon rind
⅔ cup freshly shredded coconut

Boil the milk with the shredded coconut. Cover with the tapioca mixed with the sugar and the salt the bottom of an 8-inch square glass baking dish. Pour the hot milk and coconut over the tapioca. Scatter the lemon rind on top, cover the dish and wait until the grains are soft and the tapioca is completely cold before refrigerating, about six to eight hours. If using quick-cooking tapioca it will take half the time. Cut the tapioca into two-inch squares, and cover with freshly shredded coconut.

RIO, A GOOD PLACE TO LIVE

Besides attracting a large population from all regions of the country, until 1960 the city was its capital and main political and financial center. It has assimilated several waves of migration caused by regional drought or economic hardship, and it still attracts a large number of young people. Over its many centuries, it has accumulated a concentration of various professionals in the public services and in all activities evolving from their work. Engineers; architects; broadcasting and entertainment industry professionals such as filmmakers, photographers, producers, actors, directors, journalists, and screen-writers; university students; public servants; young doctors; and lawyers and bureaucrats. The country's large multinational conglomerates— telecommunications, electricity, oil, and those in the service of these—have established their headquarters in the city.

Even after the capital transferred to Brasília in 1960, Rio kept its status as an important cultural and economic center. Today 2.5 million of its people are migrants from outside the city; half of them are from the northeast. The influence of their regional foods appears on everyday tables. One of the favorite dishes is jerked beef; the dry meat is rehydrated, braised, and served with pumpkin purée or in the typical northeastern dish, a version of Shepherd's Pie—*Escondidinho* (loosely translated as "hidden"). This is a gratin prepared with the well-seasoned braised jerked beef covered with pumpkin or cassava purée, grilled, and served with strong pepper sauce; it has acquired a cult following.

However, not all the migrants come from the northeast; one of the most influential groups is from the state of Minas Gerais, in the inland. It is a region not far from Rio, only two and a half hours by car. A mountainous state with no access to the sea, Mina Gerais was closed to outside influences for quite a few centuries and developed a rich and complex local food culture, although with an eye toward Rio as a center of reference. Theirs are the best dishes prepared with pork, the best traditional fresh and curated cheeses, guava pastes, and a glorious invention in its many different presentations—*Doce de leite*, milk marmalade.

This is not to say that foods from all the other states are not represented or at least available in the city. Until the 1970s, Cariocas would go to a restaurant to eat the sophisticated dishes from the state of Pará in the Amazon region or to taste one of the many river fishes from the inland state of Goiás, considered exotic food. At that time, a barbecue was still a food style from southern Brazil that families ate at restaurants. The barbecue prepared in backyards blends the original gaucho way of preparing meat with influence from North American family gatherings.

Historically, there was never much space for gourmet extravagances in public places unless served for men only and in cabarets. The sad truth is that gourmet food is a tiny market in Rio, but fortunately growing. Rio's very traditional society would rather go out to eat at places that assure them of the status quo rather than try adventurous novelties. Homemade food carries the idea that it is healthy and righteous—yes, there is a morality in what one chooses to eat. A young woman of good family, but not rich, during the 1920s would bring her own food to work. A rich girl would not work outside her house. Therefore, again, the home food repertoire prevailed until the end of World War II.

This myriad of differences in local flavors, plus an ingrained love for food prepared at home, enlarged a special restaurant market dedicated to simple everyday fare to eat at lunchtime. Although this chapter is dedicated to food prepared at home by immigrants and migrants, a new style of restaurant, the *Quilo* (the name means "kilogram"), that features a buffet served with a special local flavor will be presented here, as it is more a continuation of the food prepared at home.

The Quilo

The next best invention to the PF—*plat du jour*—is the Quilo, a self-service buffet with a scale at the end of the serving line. Each person chooses from a large variety of salads and hot dishes, weighs the plate, and pays for the selected amount of foods. The Quilo restaurants are not an invention of the city; military canteens serving large amounts of food for its troops for many centuries evolved into different fast-food services. One of its many advantages is that those who eat smaller amounts pays less for a meal, which eliminates a typical reason for not going to many low-priced restaurants in the city: "too much food."

Quilos filled the void left by the old boardinghouses with their home-style selection of dishes. Starting in the late 1970s, at first they attracted a younger crowd at lunch hour, but they took off in the last decade of the twentieth century when a younger generation of owners changed the traditional cold and hot dishes at the buffets, adding a sushi bar or a barbecue grill. Not all of them are good, but some are very good. Rice and beans are served every day, fish is served on Fridays—a leftover of the meatless days of the city's Catholic past.

The Quilos are an intermediary category, although they are restaurants from the commercial point of view, even when they are at the lower end of the gourmet scale. The dishes are generally understood as healthy, although almost all of them serve the delicate fried dumplings loved in the city—corn fritters, fried shrimps, fried manioc, delicate shrimp or chicken fried dumplings filled with cheese, fried dumplings—pasteis filled with hearts of palm or ground beef, and sometimes a healthy baked empanada—the typical Argentinean pie. They have all the different dishes a home should have, without the bother of cooking. In fact, the food is a substitute home food, a qualification that the PF does not have, although the food is much the same as what is usually cooked at home: rice and beans, meat plus one vegetable, with a bottle of pepper sauce and manioc flour on the table, they do not taste like home food.

Today, according to the census from 2010,[2] the majority of Rio's population ranges in age from ten to thirty years. The young parents with small

Boats resting at the fisher's co-op in Copabacana Beach, where fresh fish is sold early in the morning. *Source*: Marcia Zoladz.

children are either working or in school. Nowadays, the city has long commuting times, an average of ninety minutes a day, leaving no time at all for families to rely on traditional roles that dominated family relations until late in the twentieth century, so food at the Quilos is the best substitute for home food in many circumstances.

HOUSEHOLD ECONOMICS

Rio de Janeiro after the end of the nineteenth century started to lose its importance in Brazil's economy. By 1929, the city contributed 28 percent of the industrial output of the country, and by 1970, only 15.6 percent.[3]

It is difficult to explain how a city could remain so much in the public eye for such a long time and at the same time maintain a very financially restricted life. It was a modest life, reflected in the Cariocas' food—fresh produce and everyday-life recipes.

Plain rice

2 cups water
1 cup rice, long grain
2 tablespoons soy, corn, or canola oil
1 small onion, minced
2 garlic cloves, minced
2 teaspoons salt

Bring the water to a boil. Meanwhile, wash the rice grains in plenty of water and drain a couple of times to diminish the starch content of the grains. While the rice grains drain and the water comes to a boil, add the oil, onion, and cloves to a separate pot on low heat and braise the garlic for about a minute, until it becomes aromatic. Add the rice and stir to combine with the garlic and onions; the grains will dry. Cover the rice with the boiling water and add the salt. Bring the water back to a boil, then cover the pot and turn the heat to low. Cook for fifteen minutes. Usually, the rice will be cooked but still firm. If there is a little water in the pot, throw it away. Cover the pot, turn off the heat, and let the rice rest five minutes before serving.

Bolinho de Arroz (Rice Patties)

A traditional example of re-use in Carioca cuisine is the transformation of plain rice into delicious patties. Leftover rice, having lost its original moisture, will be easier to keep its shape while frying. Rice patties can be prepared plain or with seasonings and other ingredients such as cooked broccoli florets, or diced carrots.

2 eggs, lightly mixed
2 cups cooked rice
4 tablespoons cassava flour
½ cup breadcrumbs
½ cup grated Parmesan cheese (optional)
¼ teaspoon baking powder
Salt
Black pepper
2 tablespoons parsley, minced
Vegetable oil to fry

Mix the eggs slightly beaten together with all the other ingredients except for the oil. Use a spatula to involve all the ingredients without letting the grains of rice lose their shape. If necessary, add a little more cassava flour or breadcrumbs. Taste and adjust the amount of salt and pepper. Make small balls of approximately three centimeters with the batter—an ice cream scoop might help to make them all the same size. Fry the patties in hot oil until golden colored. This recipe makes approximately twenty patties.

Camarão com Chuchu (Tiny Prawns with Chayote)

This dish is a very good example of the workings of a household kitchen at the start of the twentieth century. It had a wonderful color combination with the pink cooked prawns and the light green chayote sprinkled green leaves of the parsley and cilantro. It is also very inexpensive. Chayote is a gourd that grows on a climbing vine and used to be quite common in backyards; it is also inexpensive at markets. Prawns when small are also inexpensive. Braised together with white rice on the side, they make a beautiful presentation of simple elegance. This dish has to be prepared with very fresh ingredients, to achieve its full flavor.

750 g tiny prawns (about 26 oz) shelled and cleaned
Juice of half a lime
Salt to taste
2 tablespoons parsley, minced
1 medium-size onion, peeled and cut in thin rings
2 large garlic cloves, minced

4 tablespoons olive oil
3 large ripe tomatoes, peeled, with seeds removed, and roughly chopped
¼ cup water, if needed
2 chayotes, peeled and cut in 1-inch pieces
Salt and freshly ground black pepper to taste
½ tablespoon cilantro leaves, minced

Season the prawns with the lime juice, salt, and parsley. Braise the onion rings and the garlic in the oil in a small casserole, add the prawns and, as soon as they are cooked, add the tomatoes. If necessary, add one quarter cup of water. Add the chayote, sprinkle with salt, pepper, and the cilantro leaves. Cover the pan and remove from the heat; otherwise, the chayote will turn too soft. Serves four.

TRADITIONAL FESTIVE FOOD

Commemorative Brazilian meals are set up with dishes distributed all over the table at the same time, without a rigid etiquette or sequence. Formal dinners were and still are usually reserved for occasions outside family life. They were an import from France, and soon attracted interest from the rural bourgeoisie, especially in the second half of the nineteenth century when the city grew and got richer from the export of coffee grains. It was a variation of the life led in the countryside. There is also another way of serving lunches and dinners at parties, midway between the traditional table full of dishes and the French service dinner. A dinner or lunch table is beautifully set, everybody will be seated around it to eat, but the food is laid out on a sideboard. Each person serves him- or herself and sits down at the table again.

Today, however, in what looks like a revival of earlier habits, dishes are presented at the dinner table, with plates, cutlery, and napkins on a side table. A table set in this style looks like a banquet in a reduced size; it radiates abundance and welcomes family and friends. At the end of the meal, desserts are set in the same way. Depending on the time of the year, the number of fruit compotes will vary, and each family has list of favorite cakes, puddings, and desserts. Some of these are worth mentioning: *Pudim de claras*, a meringue pudding with a caramel sauce, is one of the most praised ones; *quindim*, an egg yolk and grated coconut pudding is another. As one dish is prepared with the yolks and the other with the egg whites, they are usually served together. Ice creams flavored with local fruits and chocolate mousse also belong on the table, as well as a tarte Tatin or an Apple pie. Walnut cakes and chocolate cakes are served with the ice creams too.

Shrimp Bobo

A specialty from Bahia, Bobo arrived in Rio de Janeiro together with a treasure of new dishes in 1822, when due to political disturbances in Salvador, the capital of the region, many Africans were exiled or moved to the city. The recipe went through a series of adaptations; at first yams were used to thicken the broth prepared with the shrimps, and later substituted by a cassava roots purée. The oil of the *dendê* palm is used for cooking and frying in Bahia, whereas in Rio it is only used as a flavor enhancer.

1 kg (about 2¼ pounds) cassava roots
2 kg (about 4½ pounds) medium-size shrimps
Juice of 2 large limes
¼ cup vegetable oil and olive oil mixed
3 onions, minced
6 garlic cloves, thinly sliced
8 tomatoes, very ripe, peeled and diced
1 red pepper, seedless and diced
1 yellow pepper, seedless and diced
1 green pepper, seedless and diced
4 or 5 whole black peppercorns, crushed
1 lady finger pepper or ½ jalapeño, seedless and thinly sliced
250 ml (about 1 cup) coconut milk
1 or two teaspoons oil of palm
1 cup parsley, minced
1 cup chives, minced
½ cup fresh cilantro, minced
Salt to taste

A very important note: Be sure to buy the cassava type called sweet cassava. Make sure to peel them before cooking—that is where the largest amount of cyanide, a natural poison, is concentrated. The cyanide evaporates after boiling the cassava roots fifteen minutes.

This recipe when prepared in two different stages does not take too long. In the first stage, cook the peeled cassava roots just covered with water without any salt until very soft. Remove any residual fiber and mash them with the water they were cooked in. While the roots of the cassava cook, clean the shrimps and remove their shells and heads; devein them with the tip of a knife. Cook the shells and heads in very little water in a covered pan. Drain the liquid into another pan and if necessary add more water. Season the shrimps with the lime juice.

Now for the Bobo. Braise the shrimps in the oil mix, and set them aside in another dish. In the same pan where the shrimps were braised, add the onion and the garlic, when they start to brown, add the tomatoes and the peppers, always mixing with a large wooden spoon. Add the crushed black pepper and the lady finger pepper. Mix until very hot and gradually add the mashed cassava, alternating with the coconut milk. If needed, add little by little, ¼ cup water. Add the oil of palm and stir a couple of times. Return the shrimps to the pan. Sprinkle with the parsley, chives, and cilantro. Salt to taste and bring it to the table. Rice is a natural side dish or a white corn pudding. Serves 8 to 10 portions.

SMALL AND LARGE PIES

Pies—especially the very small ones, *empadinhas*, with a variety of fillings—are one of the many finger foods served at parties. Their quality is measured by their size, the smallest ones, are the more appreciated on these occasions. In the past, the thinness of the dough was also much appreciated for its elegant appearance. This porcelain thinness is easier to achieve using lard instead of butter or margarine in the dough, the high fat content making it more pliable and easier to stretch. These pies are a treat for children, and everybody wants to take some home after the party. The fillings divide opinions; there are those who swear by the shrimp with one green olive while others love the heart of palm filling, having a slight lemony taste when using fresh ones. There is also a version with ground beef and one with chicken.

The role of the large pie, *empadão*, at the dinner table and at a party buffet is closer to that of a quiche. In Rio, open pies larger than the *empadinhas* are called quiches. And just like the French ones, they are quite beloved but are part of a general menu composition. On Sundays, for instance, one might serve a roast, a large pie, rice, and a colorful salad with a good wine or a *caipirinha*.

CODFISH PREPARED IN MANY WAYS

Codfish in Brazil is sold salted and dehydrated; therefore, it needs a certain degree of attention before using. Usually the whole piece is kept in a large receptacle completely covered with water, which is changed several times over twenty-four hours to remove all the salt. Restaurants leave large pieces of codfish in steel washbasins into which water will slowly drip so its constant renewal will finally leave the fish tender and without any salt.

There is another method for tenderizing the meat. After the codfish is unsalted and boiled, its pieces rest for a couple of hours in hot milk. Most recipes will also use a large amount of olive oil without turning greasy—again, as part of the hydrating procedure, leaving the meat smooth to the bite.

As every family has its own recipe, preparation is a very coordinated act involving the family, friends, and ancestors. Many recipes carry on the way it was always done in the past, and it serves as a moment when family members remember aunt or grandmother who has passed on. There is a certain protocol to it, somewhat different from everyday dishes. As with many fish dishes, it used to be prepared on Fridays.

The meatless Friday was a religious inheritance, but today it is more associated with how much free time one has to spend in the kitchen. The leisure time association with the menu is so strong that Quilos and PF restaurants all have either codfish or fish and seafood dishes on their menus on Fridays. In the same way, Saturday is the day one eats *feijoada*, the black bean and meat stew, and Sunday used to be the day to prepare *cozido*, a Portuguese specialty where meats and vegetables are cooked in different broths. Cozido is rarely prepared nowadays, unfortunately, due to the long hours in the kitchen that it requires.

Codfish Gomes de Sá

Originally, a specialty of the city of Porto in the north of Portugal, this is a simple casserole of potatoes and codfish chunks cooked in olive oil, presented with cooked eggs and small black olives.

500 g (about 1 pound) codfish
2 onions, cut in rings
1 garlic clove
2 cups olive oil
500 g (about 1 pound) potatoes, peeled and cooked in salted water
1 bay leaf
Salt
Pepper
2 eggs, hardboiled and sliced
Black olives, small Portuguese ones
Parsley

Soak the dried and salted codfish for twenty-four hours, renewing the water at least three times. Boil the codfish for about fifteen to twenty minutes in a large pot with plenty of water. Transfer the codfish to a colander and wash it again with very hot water. Remove skin and bones, and separate the meat into chunks with the fingers; do not use a knife.

Traditionalists recommend soaking the codfish chunks for two or three hours in hot milk, but it is not obligatory. Braise the onions and the garlic clove in three tablespoons of the olive oil until the rings turns soft on the stove top in low heat, add the potatoes cut in medium-size slices, and add the codfish chunks, the bay leaf, and the rest of the olive oil. This dish is best prepared in an earthenware pan. The dish is ready when the potatoes and codfish chunks are hot and have absorbed part of the oil. Season with salt and pepper to taste. Before serving, scatter the egg slices and the olives. Sprinkle with the parsley.

THE MEANING OF A FRAGILE
RELATIONSHIP IN A HOUSEHOLD

Brazil was the last country in the world to end slavery, in 1888, and it did so quite reluctantly over the course of almost forty years. First, the Atlantic transport of captured Africans was forbidden in 1850, but that was forced upon the government, resulting from the British apprehension of all slave ships at sea, making it impossible to continue. Then, in an absurd legislation, children born of captive mothers were free; however, they could stay with their enslaved mother until they were eight years old. If the child survived, either its owner could choose to keep the child enslaved or if he decided to free the child, he had the right to ask the State for restitution of the expenses for the child's room and board. Alternatively, the child could stay enslaved until at the age of twenty-one and at that time could pay the slave owner for all the room and board of the previous years and leave as a free person. In 1885, the government issued a final law that allowed slaves age sixty or older to stop working as slaves as long as they worked for three more years for free.

Finally, slavery was completely abolished in 1888. There is always a certain curiosity to know what happened to the enslaved population living in Rio at that time. Brazil at the end of the nineteenth century had almost no industries and a very small public school system. It liberated its slaves without a plan for how to school them and integrate them into the workforce. The jobs they already had were as skilled artisans, although unpaid, or in the informal market as construction workers, carriers, nannies, housekeepers, fruit sellers, and other unskilled labor.

This situation exasperated relations inside the households, as ex-slaves were transformed into workers who had to be paid, but did not have anywhere to go and did not want to stay. Many did stay all their lives as nannies in their former slave-owning families.

It is very difficult to reproduce today the household relations of the second half of the nineteenth century, especially in the kitchen, a place where the young daughters of the house prepared for the next step in their lives as married women. Young women of wealthier families did not have to cook, but they had to know how to harmonize the large assortment of dishes that made up the Brazilian cuisine in order to ask for them to be prepared. Judging by the menu recommendations in the books of the time, they would at least learn how to tell the cook what should be served at a dinner for eight or twelve, or at a very formal dinner.

Of course, not all the families had slaves. The city had a large number of workers who not only could not afford them, but who had friends that were slaves. At the end of the century, as the abolition movement became quite strong in the cities, involving politicians and intellectuals, and was daily discussed in newspapers, new immigrants were added to this group, mostly from France, Italy, Germany, Switzerland, and the Ottoman Empire, especially from today's Lebanon and Syria. Lebanese and Syrians arrived in Rio to work in commerce, but the large majority from other nations went inland where they established a green belt and a large delicacies industry not far from the city. Many had been factory workers in Europe, with union experience that they transmitted to the locals. They encouraged new systems of work that coincided with a strong period of industrialization in Rio de Janeiro and in São Paulo, then and now the two largest cities of the country.

The rise of the middle class brought new traditions. The day in a middle-class household would start with a quick decision of what to cook for lunch and dinner. This ritual would continue in Rio until the 1970s. Most Brazilian families were very proud of their daughters and liked to show their talents for making sweet liqueurs with local fruits, a tradition kept until after World War II. With the arrival of a new and more cosmopolitan generation and the passing of older aunts and grandmothers reared at the end of the century, the tradition faded.

The generation of women in Rio born at the start of the twentieth century wished to live in the larger world. In a way, the end of slavery also opened new doors for them. They started to go to college. They could drink cocktails, which they certainly did, as books from the 1920s had recipes in its pages. Not only was the kitchen changing but the pantry too.

WHERE ARE YOU FROM? ARE YOU SWISS?

The cities in the mountains around Rio were quite attractive to Swiss and German immigrants and, in smaller numbers, of the old Austro-Hungarian Empire. The first groups arrived during the second half of the nineteenth century; they had contracts with the imperial government of Brazil to work on farms. Soon they began to repeat their own farming model with smaller properties, and quite a few were responsible for the development of the towns in the mountains around Rio de Janeiro. The average altitude being around three thousand feet, the cooler and drier weather—in winter temperatures can drop to 5 degrees Celsius (41 Fahrenheit)—allowed an easier adaptation of their traditional products. There were three such cities: Petropolis, Teresópolis, and Nova Friburgo, all producing salamis, smoked tongue, hams, and cured meats that together with their rye and whole wheat breads and delicious cookies and cakes, became highly prized by families traveling there for the weekend.

EVEN MORE IMMIGRANTS

In order to explain the arrival of immigrants from countries other than Portugal in Rio, it is necessary to understand how large groups of Europeans moved to Brazil instead of the United States or Argentina, two important centers of immigration during the second half of the nineteenth century.

The Portuguese Crown and, later, Brazilian governments throughout the nineteenth century and the start of the twentieth signed collective contracts allowing large groups to establish themselves in Brazil in prearranged areas to work in predetermined activities. The Swiss, the first group, had 261 families with 1,681 persons. They arrived in 1820, from Fribourg and were sent to Nova Friburgo, a region in the mountains to the north of Rio, the mountain chain Serra do Mar, where there are valleys and plateaus with orchards and gardens. Not all of them were farmers, but as a way out of poverty in their original land, they had accepted contracts to work as farmers on Brazilian coffee plantations. It was not a successful enterprise, however, and soon they established themselves in the town or in Rio.

The experience was repeated with a group of Germans arriving in 1824, which was more successful. First of all, they were farmers, and they were living in a rural area similar to their own on the southern frontier of Brazil. Each family received twenty-seven acres of land to cultivate. More Germans, Russians, Poles, and Italians mostly from the Veneto arrived at colonies in the south in the same small-property model. This would end up also establishing a series of towns, large plantations or large farms, and large cities, now common in central and southeast Brazil.

The second wave of immigrants came to Brazil under an ill-fated concept that slaves on large coffee plantations in the state of São Paulo could be replaced by European farm laborers. As the Brazilian imperial government well understood that slavery would soon end, an immigration contract was established with the Veneto region in today's northern Italy. The immigrants started to arrive in 1870, and their number grew steadily, with 515,533 arriving in the decade from 1884 to 1893, and another 537,784 in the next decade.[4]

This second kind of contract was different. These groups arrived much later, after the Italian unification in 1870, and they came to work as laborers on the coffee farms inland from São Paulo. However, this area had a large plantation economy based on slave work, lacking adequate lodgings and adequate agricultural equipment, and it would not willingly letting go of the old model. Therefore, a large number of the immigrants would leave for the towns close to the farms or to São Paulo.

As often happens when people are escaping famine, the Brazilian immigrants tended to accept any offered job. But such contracts had problems on both sides, for the farmers did not always honor their contracts, offering terrible working conditions, and on the other side, quite often many of the newly arrived were from cities, and they soon left the farms to work in occupations they really wanted or knew. Their internal migration was very important for the country, as they founded new cities and introduced multiple possibilities of life. In the end, however, the initial concept of immigration as a way of acquiring new and inexpensive farm hands failed, since the problem lay with the archaic and absurd production system of the farms.

Immigrants started to arrive in larger numbers early in the twentieth century, not only to Rio, but also to the states of Amazon and Pará, in the north of the country. They came from the Ottoman Empire, the Russian Empire, Central Europe, Germany, and the north of Italy. They had different religions—Orthodox Christians, Oriental Jews, Catholics, Lutherans, Calvinists, and Presbyterians, which added to the local religious life and the Catholic traditions. Each of these groups brought new ingredients and dishes to the country, which can now be found for sale in the greenmarkets of Rio.

The Japanese government also had a similar immigration contract in 1907, and from the newly arrived 75 percent went to the state of São Paulo. Today there are approximately 1.5 million Brazilians of Japanese ancestry. Before the Japanese arrived, nobody ate fresh tuna in Rio. They also introduced new varieties of turnips, larger tomatoes, and different lettuces.

Just as important as their food traditions, newly arriving immigrants injected a new strength into the economy and a variety of life styles that transformed the contemporary eating habits of the Brazilians. The Germans started apple, pear, and peach orchards in the state of Santa Catarina. The Italians developed a powerful grape juice and wine industry; they also brought their own food, but in a very creative way, they further developed what they found in the country. New businesses, such as sweets and the chocolate industry, also sprang up in Rio and other cities.

KIBBEH, A VERY BRAZILIAN DISH

At the end of the Ottoman Empire in 1918, a new wave of immigrants started to arrive from the Middle East. Although they had been coming since the late nineteenth century, it was during the twentieth century that their contribution to the food in the city enlarged the list of traditional and beloved dishes of the Carioca's table. Each immigration wave from the Middle East added new cultural influences in different ways. The first to arrive, dubbed Turks, arrived from North Africa and the Middle East carrying passports from the Ottoman Empire. After World War I, many came from Armenia; however, the majority were from Syrian and Lebanese families, and they were Jews and Orthodox Christians, very few Muslims.

A large number of the Middle Eastern émigrés arrived before World War II, escaping poverty, lack of work, and religious persecution, as in the case of Jews. Many were urban professionals and business owners arriving from cities such as Cairo, Beirut, and Alexandria. Some of them came with a strong cultural influence from the British or French protectorate in their homeland, and so spoke other languages besides Arabic.

They worked at first in commercial venues, most opening stores and restaurants in the same neighborhood in the city center, which is still today called the Sahara. Their contributions reinvigorated the Brazilian economy, and also changed the nature of street food in the city from its nineteenth-century tradition of *angú* and *acarajés* from Bahia to *sfihas* from Lebanon filled with vegetables and Brazilian fresh cheese instead of their traditional cheeses made from sheep or goat's milk. They also served fried and baked kibbehs prepared with ground beef instead of lamb, introduced new breads, and imported Middle Eastern dried fruits and nuts. In addition, they added to the already existing practice of large generous tables with their mezzes—small portions of traditional dishes served as appetizers that fit perfectly with the local habit of drinking cold beers and having long chats around a table.

Today in Rio, "Arabic food," as it is usually called, means a light and nutritious dish, especially because the dishes are presented in smaller portions with healthy ingredients—salads, rice mixed with lentils, grape leaves or cabbage stuffed with rice and meat, hummus, and baba ghanoush. Syrian-style curd is also much appreciated. These foods are so well integrated into the local kitchen that they are sold in large supermarket chains, produced either by major brands or in higher-end versions for traditional rotisseries and sophisticated deli stores. Kibbeh, for instance, is sold in its standard size or in bite-size packages. Sfihas can be found with chicken or filled with spinach, and open sfihas have ground beef or za'atar.

The Middle Eastern groups also introduced bulgur in Brazil; it is so well adapted in the local kitchen that it can be bought in large supermarket chains as wheat for kibbeh, although it is also used in the tabbouleh salad. Middle Eastern dishes in Brazil are a generalization of regional foods from the region, as many dishes are common to both Jewish and Christian Orthodox communities.

Baked Kibbeh, Brazilian Style

The original kibbeh recipe had to be adapted by Middle Eastern immigrants, since quite a few of the original ingredients were not available. Pine nuts are rare in Brazil and therefore expensive, so they were soon left out of the recipe. Maybe their slight bitterness also was a factor in a culture that does not favor either bitter or sour flavors. Lamb meat in Brazil is not so easy to find in local markets, either; it usually has to be preordered, or one has to go to a special butcher, which leaves it restricted usually to festive occasions where one would prepare a shank of lamb for roasting, but more rarely ground into meat balls for kibbeh.

Brazilian-style fried kibbeh prepared with ground beef. *Source*: Marcia Zoladz.

The Brazilian baked version of kibbeh consists of two layers of well-seasoned ground beef mixed with bulgur, with a softer middle layer with meat only and a large amount of seasonings.

For the middle layer or filling:

1 onion, diced
2 tablespoons canola or soy oil
½ pound ground beef
Salt and black pepper to taste
Cinnamon, a small pinch

For the upper and lower layers:

1 pound ground beef
½ cup fine bulgur (called tabbouleh wheat)
1 onion, diced
½ teaspoon salt
½ teaspoon black pepper

At the end add:

2 tablespoons pine puts or almonds cut into two or three pieces
2 tablespoons olive oil
½ cup water or broth

Let the bulgur sit covered in water overnight; it will swell and increase in volume. Next day, drain the bulgur well in a colander.

Prepare the middle layer first. Braise the onion in the oil; add the meat, season with salt, pepper, and the pinch of cinnamon. Cook only lightly, as it will finish cooking in the oven.

Prepare the upper and lower layers by mixing the meat with the bulgur and the onion; season with salt and pepper (sometimes a little parsley is mixed in as well).

Lightly grease the bottom and the sides of an ovenproof baking dish with olive oil; spread half the meat and bulgur mixture on the bottom of the dish. Spread the middle layer over the bottom layer and cover with the other half of the meat and bulgur mixture.

Score the surface with diagonal lines, drawing diamond shapes, and press one pine nut or almond piece at the center of each. Drizzle with the olive oil and with the water. Bake in preheated oven at 200° C (400° F) until golden brown, around 35 minutes. To prevent the kibbeh from frying in the baking pan add more water or broth after twenty minutes.

A Note on Acarajé and Kibbeh

It is very difficult to trace the travels of individuals before they arrived in Brazil, although the routes where the slaves groups usually started, where they stopped, and where the several trade fairs took place on their way to the coast to embark to the Americas are documented. But there is a collective group knowledge that translated itself into agricultural techniques, the adaptation of plants, and in recipes.

Africans brought with them many recipes, but one is especially beloved: *acarajé*, a dumpling deep-fried in dendê oil, prepared with a soft batter prepared with black-eyed peas. The dumpling migrated from Bahia to Rio during the nineteenth century. Acarajés may be filled with an okra dip, *caruru*, or with a dried shrimp and peanuts dip, *vatapá*, of Afro-Brazilian origin. Sometimes they are rolled quite small, bite size, to be served at parties.

Because of this earlier and very successful introduction of new fried foods, the population readily accepted the kibbeh. When the immigration from the Middle East began, the city already had a list of deep-fried homemade dumplings in its dishes; especially beloved were—and are—the ones prepared with rice.

In its fried version, kibbeh has an outer crust made with softened bulgur and ground beef surrounding a filling of seasoned meat. Both dumplings, acarajé and kibbeh, added another technique to the kitchens in Rio. They freed Carioca's from the porridges and soups of the Portuguese dishes, introducing new textures to the palate.

HERRINGS WITH CREAM

World War II started another layer of cultural changes. This time the newly arrived had a different experience, they were running for their lives, having barely survived. Among these people were a large number of Jews, especially from Eastern Europe. A certain number of displaced persons were young people whose families had died. They all had a strong urge to build a new life.

There were also non-Jews from the same Central and Eastern European countries affected by the war: Rumania, Bulgaria, Poland, Czechoslovakia, Slovenia, and Hungary. They brought to the city something very new, having had a cosmopolitan life before the war, with multiple influences and a rich intellectual exchange. They were not rich; they arrived poor, having left behind their businesses under special conditions, but they were professionally well qualified, and in a few years, many were able to achieve middle-class status. Socializing at bars and restaurants became more sophisticated, more related to an international menu, as Europeans mingled with their new Brazilian friends.

They arrived for a new life just when the city needed them to create a modern lifestyle. The ten years after the end of World War II were crucial in reshaping the cultural life and therefore the food in the city. New business, new shops, and new department stores sprang up. Sears Roebuck opened a huge store in a new modern building in 1949. There were old Brazilian department stores, such as Mesbla, started in 1912, as well as many other department stores, selling sewing machines, home appliances, bedding, clothes, jewelry—all with a restaurant in the last floor. These stores were based on Selfridges or Marks & Spencer, the British department stores, and more than one specialized in elegant ladies' apparel from hats and gloves to clothes, perfumes, and beauty products.

The arrival of this newer generation with its more varied experience of retail shopping changed the traditional market in Brazil, enlarging it. Many of the Jewish immigrants, especially those who had lived in larger cities before the war, had worked in elegant stores and they had a different work experience than the one they initially found in Rio. Buying food was part of the shopping experience that also started to change. The way younger women tried to organize their married life influenced the consumer market at the end of the 1950s, when new products started to be sold with newly designed packages and a new dynamic advertising language for television.

In 1966, it was possible to buy a Sacher torte or a strawberry cake at a German, Austrian, or Hungarian pastry shop. The large number of immigrants turned the apple strudel into a common dessert, served in many restaurants around the city. Many years later, when the owners of the restaurants retired, their old employees took over the business. And here again we see the ability of the Carioca to take a new dish into the culture and its everyday life: Strudels today can be bought frozen in many sweet and savory flavors in the supermarkets; there is even a codfish-filled one.

Another typical snack served at bakeries and coffeehouses is named after a city where the imperial family lived part of year. Petropolis Toast consists of two thick toasted slices of brioche bread spread with lots of butter and cut into three or four vertical slices—very comforting with a cup of coffee and milk or tea. Petropolis, located in the mountains close to Rio, attracted a number of German and northern Italian immigrants with its cooler climate. The immigrants opened a number of small businesses, producing breads, comfits, and chocolates soon sold in the city and later in the coffeehouses in Rio.

Eastern Europeans came mostly from small towns and settled in downtown Rio; closer to the end of the 1930s more immigrants from German-speaking countries began to arrive. There were not many Jewish restaurants with Kosher food in the city—although there were butchers, deli stores, and catering services for parties and marriages. Later, the communities went to live in several different areas, either south or north of the city center.

Just to give an example, in the 1950s, maybe earlier, it was possible to buy at a Viennese deli store some herring with smetana—sour cream—and a German-style rye bread and eat it with raw onion and tomatoes, a typical combination from Central and East Europe. The herring was probably replaced by sardines, which are easier to find in Rio, but they were very finely pickled. Smetana has all but disappeared from menus now, I suspect more from the passing of first- and second-generation immigrants and new fad diets in the 1970s that took over the everyday food culture of the city. One can still eat smetana at one of the multiple German restaurants, mostly as an accompaniment for apple strudel, but it is not very common.

IN THE SUMMER IT SIZZLES, A NOTE ON THE HEAT

One of the main difficulties for a European immigrant in a city like Rio is the heat. At the height of the summer sometimes the temperature reaches 55° C (131° F). It is very, very hot. Therefore there is a constant need to eat light and refreshing foods. However, some eating habits are so ingrained that some dishes are served year 'round. There are more salads on the table, one drinks more water, and ice creams and ice-cold mate are part of the summer foods, but at the same time everybody keeps eating rice and beans. Mate (*Ilex paraguaiensis*), is a native plant drunk cold in Rio de Janeiro, completely different from its traditional hot counterpart in South Brazil, Uruguay, Argentina, Paraguay, and Chile. Eating healthy food to counteract tropical diseases still today is an important part of the food served at home or in restaurants.

IPANEMA

In the 1950s a new sound started to play on the radio. It was a soft sound with a leisurely beat, a music so sophisticated it soon attracted great musicians from all over the world. As the bossa nova flourished on the airwaves, a new generation of young men and teenagers took to the waves of the Beach of Ipanema with their surfboards. A new group of people with a new lifestyle and eating parameters arriving from the Orient—macrobiotic diet, yoga as an exercise—were searching for a life more integrated with nature. They introduced new salads, whole-grain rice, the use of unsweetened cocoa in cakes, tofu, and soy sauce, and they made Japanese cuisine everyday food on the Carioca's table.

The first restaurants of this type were small vegan or macrobiotic shops where it was possible to buy everything from books to whole-grain rice, to surfer-style shirts. This lifestyle was well attuned with the geography of the city, with its beaches and mountains. This new food with an influence from Asia coincided with a new foreign influence arriving from California and Hawaii in the United States—the surf generation. In the new century all these influences are firmly established in a list of ingredients, many borrowed from Chinese and Japanese cuisine. Soy sauce, tofu, different chards, ginger root, and sesame mix with the Amazonian assai and Western food and make for a varied and healthy diet.

Chapter Four

Markets and Retailing

As a large harbor, Rio's activities evolved in the course of its four hundred fifty years. At first it was engaged in supplying ships on their way to India and exporting agricultural goods. The need to supply the ships developed other activities around the maritime industry, including preparing food for the ships and providing for the population involved in harbor-related activities. The city, an import and export center until the end of the nineteenth century, eventually lost its primacy to Santos in the state of São Paulo, especially because of the export of coffee. Its port activities did not end, however, as cereals continued arriving from faraway countries such as Russia and Poland, and wines and olive oil from Portugal. It was also a constant commercial partner with other cities of the country, which shipped their goods to the capital and its larger consumer market. The harbor thus continued to be an important part of the supply chain for the local inhabitants and for travelers.

It is important to understand that for a city like Rio, which started its urban growth as part of the colonial business and was completely involved in its activities as a port, it was natural to develop an interest in the novelties arriving from abroad, food included. Therefore, after a while, these products that came from the outside—olives, wines, preserves, fine chocolates, liqueurs—took on a cachet of quality and ended by mixing with the local dishes together with the local food offered to its citizens by specialty stores.

As the colonial business grew, so did the knowledge of techniques in agriculture, some products improved from almost inedible to staples on everybody's table. Good examples are potatoes and tomatoes. Others, like corn, spread to other countries, mostly in southern Europe. There was a better assortment of dried meats, better wines, better sherry, the introduction of rum, of *cachaça* in the seventeenth century, and the success of Madeira, a fortified wine that loved the heat of the tropical weather. All these improve-

The Fortress of Santa Cruz at the entrance of the Guanabara Bay. *Source*: Marcia Zoladz.

ments together with the export of sugar and coffee turned Rio into a rich city, with a rich harbor.

THE FIRST SUPPLY LIST

The list of ingredients and prepared food supplies for sale in a city like Rio during its colonial period, until 1808, was adapted according to the needs of its main buyers, the ships that stopped in the harbor. Travel on the Atlantic Ocean and crossing the tropics in hot weather was hard on the bodies—and stomachs—of the seamen. The wooden hulls of the ships did not provide a properly sealed environment, and food was stocked in conditions that contributed to fouling the water, souring the wine, deteriorating any flour and rotting the biscuits used as bread substitute, attracting small insects and rats. A ship usually departed with a good stock of these items. Crews would sometimes bring their own food items too, varying according to rank and nationality. It is easy to imagine a doctor or a captain with a special bottle of port wine or a nice pie of hare meat at the start of the trip.

The choice of foods was limited by their longevity. Some of the more constant items were almonds, fava beans, garlic, onions, sugar, honey, and rice. Meat for the trip was usually salted, smoked, or dried; it could be either beef, pork, or lamb for a trip embarking from Lisbon. Lard was used for cooking but also for storage of meat and eggs. Cooked meat when completely submerged in fat vats, with its oxygen supply decreased, allows for a longer storage period. Dried and salted cod was a constant in the Portuguese navy diet. Sometimes a cow and chickens would be taken on board to provide milk and eggs.

There were, however, some delights during the Atlantic crossing, the discovery of the ocean itself being one of them, at least for the many scientific explorers during the eighteenth century. As we can see by the description of Sir Joseph Banks, a fellow traveler aboard Captain Cook's *Endeavor*.

> 1768 September 25. Wind continued to blow much as it had done so we were sure we were well in the trade; now for the first time we saw plenty of flying fish, whose bea[u]ty especialy when seen from the cabbin windows is beyond imagination, their sides shining like burnishd silver; when seen from the Deck they do not appear to such advantage as their backs are then presented to the view, which are dark colourd."[1]

A voyage to India could last half a year, and upon arrival the crew and passengers would find a climate to which they were completely unadjusted. Some did not last the whole year. To enhance the dissemination of European foods, travelers brought with them very early on fig trees, grapes vines, and trees and herbs with medical properties.

A prepared piece of codfish served with cooked potatoes. *Source*: Marcia Zoladz.

There were strategic stops where the ships would leave sick sailors or captains would let their crews rest; the island of Saint Helena was one of them. Located off the coast of South Africa, Portuguese and British ships stopped there on their way back to Europe, after the difficult crossing of the Cape, or on their way to India from Rio de Janeiro. It was an uninhabited rock in the middle of the South Atlantic; there was water but almost no vegetation, and yet they left goats, sheep, and rabbits there, and planted fruits.

In the seventeenth and eighteenth centuries, rations were part of the payment of the crews. When people complained, it meant that whatever was presented before them was completely rotten, foul-smelling, and infested with vermin. It was a life surrounded by sickness and pests.

Perhaps the bad quality of food is not very hard to understand. Naval companies would move the leftover food cargo from a ship just arrived in Lisbon or other European harbor to another ready to set sail, even if the items were rotten and would get even worse during the new trip. It was partly the miserly thinking of the merchant companies, but on the other hand, in the colonial world, nobody knew about viruses and bacteria or washing their hands when cooking or serving food. However, the large toll of lives began to induce the colonial businesses to search for remedies. One of the first was the use of fresh oranges and other fresh citrus fruits to avoid scurvy, a disease caused by lack of vitamin C. Soon citrus trees were bearing fruits in the harbors where fleets stopped for supplies, all the way to India. In 1820, quinine, extracted from the bark of the Cinchona tree, a native plant from Peru, was isolated as a remedy for malaria.

SUPPLIES IN RIO

Arriving in Rio meant surviving a hard trip and reaching a fresh source of food supplies. Some of them were quite basic ones for survival, such as water, dried and smoked meats, dried and salted fish, salt, and rum or cachaça and these were resupplied during the trip. With time, every stop started to provide local specialties. Providing food for all the ships traveling to other Portuguese colonies in Africa and India was sometimes a problem for Rio; in Brazil there was no wheat, for instance, so cassava toasts, or *beijus*, were substituted for biscuits. Early on, ships sometimes had to wait for a couple of months for a crop of peas or beans.

The city had three hundred thousand inhabitants in 1700 and two main activities. One was its harbor and all the shipyard activities, including providing supplies to the ships, which also required an extended network of farms, various orchards, foragers, cattle raisers, butchers, millers, bakers, and fishermen. The second one was the export of sugar, cotton, indigo, gold, and coffee.

The Jesuit order of the Catholic Church gives a good example of the workings of the supply system. The Jesuits had large cattle farms in Rio and were successful rice planters. They also had large orchards and produced different fruit marmalades for export. With private harbors and great wealth and being exempt from taxes for the import and export of their merchandise, they and their neighbors, other Catholic orders in the Bay of Sepetiba region, were an important part of the food supply chain in the city. The Jesuits remained a powerful economic group until their expulsion from all the Portuguese colonies, including Brazil, and from Portugal in 1759. They came back later, in 1841, but under different political circumstances, mainly as educators, building schools and colleges.

The whole supply effort was concentrated in Rio's export business, as was the feeding of government employees and the inhabitants of other cities in Brazil, even rich ones located in the gold and diamond districts of Minas Gerais, who had to eat only what was local and possible to grow or pay a high price for goods brought in. A good example of the precedence of the government officials over the civilian population is in a letter Domingos José Gomes wrote to his cousin from Rio, in July 1778, informing him that there were no wine caskets in the storages to send him the wine, as the captain of the troops had requested them. They would have to wait for the arrival of a ship from Porto, Portugal.[2]

Goods arrived on the backs of donkeys, traveling long distances on very poor roads. As a consequence, strategic stops along the way helped to establish cities inland. Later each one of them started to develop local agriculture-related businesses on a larger scale. In Rio there were the cassava plantations making flour and *beiju*, oven-dried biscuits prepared with the same cassava roots used to make flour. Lard came all the way from Cunha, 180 kilometers (112 miles) south of Rio. Salt was imported from Portugal; the first sea salt extraction region in Brazil was only established in Cabo Frio, 152 kilometers (94.4 miles) north of Rio, in 1823.

With the Brazilian independence from Portugal, inserted into the international business community after three hundred years of colonial domination, Rio in 1822 was a busy merchant city with a desirable market. French, Germans, British, and Italians all wanted to export merchandise and also to import goods from Europe, from clocks to pianos to fine wines and fine cured meats; everything that belonged in a modern economy was available.

In addition to the supply of food and related items to passing fleets on their way to India, another activity of the harbor was the export of agriculture products and, during the eighteenth century, the export of gold. Until 1808, the Portuguese Crown viewed Brazil as a captive market for its products, but after that date, the ports opened to all friendly nations; therefore, a larger amount of goods from different places started to arrive in the country.

RIO AND MODERN DEVELOPMENTS

Food at sea and the fulfillment of orders for the kitchens changed definitely for the better with the introduction of the new ships with steam engines after 1840. The introduction of new iron hulls gave crossing the oceans a new meaning. A trip from Lisbon that before would take two and a half months took two weeks with the new steam engines by the end of the nineteenth century, and this vastly improved the storage conditions. Cargoes crossing the oceans faster accelerated merchandise exchange and made it more reliable, allowing for new business opportunities and the importing of a greater variety of ingredients that the country could not produce.

The city kept its tradition as a large food supplier for ships well into the twentieth century, but it was completely outpaced by refrigerators and airplanes, not exactly in that order, but both contributed in the decline of harbor activities. The usual stop to refill inventories of supplies in Rio was less necessary, as ships could stay for longer times at sea. Refrigerators, or rather cold rooms, allowed for a complete change in the diet at sea.

Ocean liners' kitchens turned the experience of crossing the Atlantic into a voyage similar to a stay in a hotel. Cargo and warship crews started to eat the same style of food as their colleagues at bases and ports. Airplanes reduced the number of regular ship passengers to almost none. At the same time, airplanes helped ocean cruiser companies build stronger brands, enhancing the quality of their products and making it more uniform. One sort of wine, from one single place, can be on the menu of different ships of the same company at the same time in cities far from one another. And salmon can travel daily from the cold Patagonian waters where they are raised to all the fish markets of the world, Rio being no exception.

As airplanes changed transportation, a large highway network built during the 1970s also replaced the smaller boats that brought food to the city. The city had separated its productive life from the harbor. The import and export activity of food merchants was not so important for the Carioca table, with the exception *bacalhau*—dried codfish—and Portuguese wines. As their identity started to look to the local produce, elegance meant eating manioc flour, finding local fruits for dessert, and inviting friends to eat shrimps baked inside a pumpkin.

A HOUSE WITH A GARDEN

Until the nineteenth century, the local population in the city ate the same foods they produced to supply the ships, plus some local specialties—stewed beans; dried meats; some local vegetables adapted from African, Portuguese, and Amerindian kitchens; and cassava flour, a constant in their tables.

A reliable source of food for the population was the backyard garden. It was there that it was possible to experiment with adapting new plants and vegetables and to establish a closer relationship with the tropical climate. The backyard, *os quintais*, also became part of the lifestyle. It was the place where children played, where fruits were sorted for jams and liqueurs, and herbs were gathered for teas and syrups against colds or infections. More important than its use as a workplace, it was where all the informal social gatherings took place.

It is also in this backyard full of trees that music was and still is played. One of the birthplaces of the samba in 1916 was the backyard of Tia Ciata, a well-known personality in Rio. She was also one of the leaders of the Afro-Brazilian religion of her time. Gatherings on weekends developed important cultural traits in the life of the city; for example, one of the many styles of the samba—*partido alto*—is played together, and each visitor defies the other with verses and music. The other cultural trait is the love of small and tasty tidbits. While the music is played there is the a never-ending sequence of small savories—fried fish, fried liver sticks with onions, fried sausages—served to the guests, originally with cachaça, and today with fruit *caipirinhas* and very cold beer.

It is difficult to establish the precise amount of fruits, vegetables, and meat—usually poultry and pork—that households produced in their back-yards during the nineteenth century, but they should not be dismissed as an unimportant supply source. The backyards were responsible for the introduction of a large number of new plants and fruits that later were planted on a larger scale. They obviously supplemented the family diet in a less expensive way than shopping at a street food market or store, but they were also very valued at meals and were part of a constant exchange, as some recipes in notebooks named after aunts and friends bear testimony. They were a source of a large variety of ingredients to the everyday table if one considers all the items listed in the book *Jardineiro Brazileiro*.

According to this book, published in 1914, there were 111 different kinds of vegetables, and 120 fruit trees. The book also has a list of cough syrups and medical infusions with herbs, and it gives advice on the best way to prepare meats.

Ordinarily, ingredients were bought at markets and specialized shops; however, the city was not that large and did not have a strict separation between its urban and agricultural activities. A family of modest means living in the city would have a small orchard and a couple of hens for their own use well into the twentieth century. Only after World War II when existing houses in different regions of the city gave way to apartment buildings did the backyard lose its importance. By then, weekly green markets were organized

and had become part of a new lifestyle, especially in the southern region close
to the beaches.

This change raised homemade marmalades and compotes into a specialty—*doces caseiros*. Homemade sweets gained a new and rather flattering
status as gourmet desserts, especially those made and brought from Minas
Gerais, and they had higher standing if they came from a friend's or relative's farm. They are indeed very special when they achieve the right level of
sweetness while at the same time keep the whole taste of the fruit. Families
with larger orchards made their guava paste a precious gift, cherished, and
recommended and envied by family members and friends.

A small ordinary backyard for the Cariocas would have one or two vegetable beds with pumpkins; green beans; climbers such as chayote and peas;
green kale; spinach; taioba (*Xantoshoma sagittifolium*); seasonings such as
chives, parsley, and cilantro; and one or two medicinal plants for a tisane,
lemongrass was a favorite and mint. Sometimes pennyroyal was planted in
a vase in order to restrain its growth. One bush of small malagueta peppers
would also be there. Fruit trees were part of the backyard as well, either to
provide fresh fruit or for compotes, jams, or marmalades. A common selling
point for a house was if it had a jabuticaba or mango tree in the backyard, but
quinces, pitangas, guavas, lemons, bananas, figs, peaches, or pears could also
be found. Backyards in the older houses might have three or four trees, all
producing fruits. One of them might be a jack tree, not always liked because
of their strong smell; they also attracted small monkeys and fruit-eating bats,
and when the ripe fruits crashed open on the ground, they spread a gluey sap.

GREEN MARKETS

The traditional way, or rather the apparently disorganized way, of selling
vegetables, fruits, milk and cakes, poultry, fish, or any kind of goods in the
streets of the city, was only possible because in the early days the area was
very small and densely inhabited. The old part of downtown was the whole
city, accessed, then as now, by foot. Small squares in front of churches and
public buildings, offered the perfect place to stop and buy food or refresh-
ments. Many of these places disappeared as the city grew and reorganized,
and now some of the old churches stand at the very edge of the street, without
sidewalks.

Early on, slaves and private sellers sold fresh food in the streets. Women had
a right to this practice as a way of maintaining themselves and their families.
Later, the city officials started to offer a series of services for the ever-increasing
number of hotels and restaurants, establishing a centralized food distribution

Tatooed woman selling cashews in the streets of Rio de Janeiro. *Source*: Watercolor on paper by Jean-Baptiste Debret, 1827, Wikimedia Commons, https://commons.wiki media.org/wiki/File%3ADebret_negra_vendendo_caju.jpg.

system similar to the one existing in Les Halles in Paris. Built in 1841, the new building was part of a reorganization of the urban model, a big change from the impoverished old colonial city. The fish market, however, with its disorderly stalls, remained where it was, which was quite close to the new building.

In 1885, the city officials tried to better organize the fish market, locating the fish stalls close to the docks so they would receive their supplies directly from the fishermen at their own docking pier. These stalls were privately owned and had to be rented, which gave rise to huge protests, but the fish market was finally organized.

The central market building engendered a huge urbanization of the city; part of the building, with its iron rotunda, still remains. In the place of the old market, new buildings and new avenues were built and old houses came down. New legislation established laws to protect the city from yellow fever and forbade milk to be sold door to door directly from a cow, as it was a health hazard.

The outdoor green markets spread to new residential neighborhoods, where they remain to this day, competing against large supermarket chains and smaller fruit and vegetables sellers. It took quite a while to regularize the activities of these markets. The first official *feira-livre*—the name means "free

"Silver" bananas, *bananas prata*, one of the many different kinds sold at street stands in the city. *Source*: Marcia Zoladz.

market"—opened with eighty stalls at Botafogo Beach on April 17, 1914. It was probably an urgent need, as food sellers were setting up their stalls all over the city, representing a constant menace to public health.

A green market offered approximately the same products they do today: fruits, vegetables, roots, potatoes, herbs, fresh seafood, salted meats, cod, dried fruits, and eggs. Then as today, they remain a point of reference for food quality and freshness.

The central market today, CADEG, was constructed in 1962. It is one of the best places to buy and eat codfish dishes in town. They have a few small restaurants where they serve large, generous portions of codfish cooked in tomato sauce with boiled potatoes.

ABOUT MEAT, PIGS, BIRDS, AND EGGS

The Portuguese who arrived to colonize Rio were from the inland of Portugal, and a large number were not city dwellers but small farmers who ate meat and drank milk, habits they introduced to the city life.

Goats, cows, and chickens arrived together with the first settlers. These were easy to take care, and a family might own one cow, just for the milk and cheese, and maybe a couple of pigs and goats. Goat's milk was thought to be less aggressive to the body and was used for babies who rejected their mother's milk. These animals were a small source of extra income. They were easy to tend, to kill, and to sell.

Pigs were killed early in the morning, before the heat of the day started, leaving time to cut the animal up and process the meat either for curing or drying. Piglets were a delicacy, served on special occasions, quite often sent already baked to the house of a relative with the head still attached to the body and the skin *pururuca*, very crisp.

At Christmastime, a turkey would be purchased a few days before. The turkey would stay in the backyard, eating corn and herbs in order to gain a little weight and to be completely cleaned out of any food it might have eaten before arriving. Then, three days before Christmas, they would give him cachaça, quite a lot of it in small amounts during the day, so the bird would be very drunk and not under any stress when the cook came by and broke its neck. Next, after a swift slice of its neck, it hung upside down to be bled. After the feathers were plucked, the skin was seared over a fire, and the bird was covered with parsley and placed in a huge bowl with wine, olive oil, onions, salt, and garlic—but first a few violent stabs guaranteed the mixture would penetrate a little further inside the meat.

The next day, very early in the morning, someone would take the bird to the bakery; gas stoves at home were small and the wood-burning ovens were needed to bake Christmas cakes. Later, the turkey presented at the table was golden brown and glorious, even if a little dry. It could be served with a nice farofa on the side and rice, or with a dried fruits stuffing; there was a wetter sort of farofa, also prepared with cassava flour, in Brazilian houses, and stale bread in the Portuguese.

A Note about Poultry

Considering the large variety of recipes for poultry in the cookbooks of one hundred years ago, the choices in the city today are far fewer. Even if not all of them were available all year around, they could be bought at markets and retailers. Many people also had coops in their backyards. The list mentioned chicken, old hens, cocks, capons, guinea fowls, pigeons, partridges, quails, ducks and teals, and turkeys. There are also interesting sorts of wild birds, macucos, tinamous, saracuras, aramides, and small birds caught with a sling. *O cozinheiro nacional*[3] also has a large number of suggestions on how to prepare them. A goose could be served with hearts of palm, a duck with quince or a certain type of elephant-ear leaf—taioba—each one of them braised or grilled, with their cavities filled with yams or plums.

Today, you can find organic-fed chickens, with or without their skins, whole or in pieces. But it is impossible to know their breed; therefore, it is impossible to know their flavor, how they were fed, making it impossible to prepare a real *coq au vin*, and even less grandmother's chicken broth. There are no geese, pigeons, turkeys, ducks, teals, pheasants, and partridges in supermarkets as there were in the backyard coops. Supermarkets killed the habit of eating different birds prepared according to old recipes in cookbooks and notebooks.

About Christmastime, it gets a little better with the arrival of the turkeys and something called a chester—a chicken especially engineered to have a very large breast, supposedly the preferred part of any poultry according to some marketing research. One wonders why, as the breast is the least succulent part of a chicken.

Red Meat

Cattle arrived in Brazil together with the first settlers; the Portuguese Crown encouraged their export to Brazil, and soon the animals were adapted to the

Typical spit roasted chicken are sold at bakeries in Rio de Janeiro. *Source*: Marcia Zoladz.

land. John Luccock, an English merchant who lived in the country from 1808 until 1818, noticed that animals sometimes would be herded to Rio from six hundred to one thousand miles away. They left behind a large number of complaints from unhappy farmers who were obliged to give right of way to the herds and had their roads trampled and their grass eaten without any payment. Traditional cattle slaughterhouses remained on the outskirts of the city, where the old monastic orders had their farms, in Santa Cruz, until the 1970s, when they became outdated and were closed.

The large cattle ranches and the beef industry today is located in the central and western states of Goiás and Mato Grosso do Sul and in the south of Brazil. These new farming areas, developed with the export market in mind, introduced better grass, new breeds, and modern completely refrigerated factories at the same time that the supermarket chains started to grow in the country. At that time, the sanitation exigencies of the importers bettered the quality of the meat products in the country, offering a larger choice of cuts, these higher-quality meats arriving at the market in large cities, meant the quality of the meat on the whole by the start of the 1980s was better controlled, and with a higher standard. Brazil today is the third-largest beef exporter of beef in world, behind India and Australia.

The butcher's counter survived the transition to the supermarket chains, where besides choosing a cut of meat from the freezer it is possible to consult with a professional and ask for special orders for a party. Small butcher's shops also are located all over the city, selling all kinds of beef and pork and sometimes lamb, rabbit, and veal. And they are more likely to sell offal: oxtail, kidneys, liver, pig's feet, hearts, and all such delicacies.

There are also boutiques for the aficionados. They sell special cuts to a prime market, sometimes meat imported from Argentina and Uruguay, but also bought from the same ranches that export to Europe. They sell different sauces, seasonings, and all the needed equipment for amateur cooks. This market received a boost at the start of the new century when the city expanded to the west, and most of the new buildings in the neighborhood of Barra da Tijuca started to feature, as a marketing appeal, a large veranda with a brick barbecue grill and a small kitchen.

BREAD IN RIO

Baking bread until the second half of the nineteenth century was a feminine occupation. Women used to make breads at home and sell them in the streets or deliver them to houses and restaurants. There were also small bakeries, such as the one opened in 1815 by a Frenchman, which was successful enough to become the official bread provider for the imperial family. The bakery, then called Padaria Rafael after its owner, existed until 1889.

A big change occurred in the country at the start of the twentieth century after a new group of Portuguese immigrants arrived who controlled the whole chain, from importing the wheat to making the flour to baking and selling the breads. By offering a lighter bread baked and delivery several times a day, they soon controlled the market. In the next century and a half, bakeries enlarged their activities from places where only breads were sold to become rotisseries, also selling cakes, sweets, ice creams, and beverages. The more traditional ones have a vertical oven where chicken rotate on a spit in front of the customers.

Thus, the concept of what a bakery should sell sometimes is a little confusing in Rio, as there is an overlapping of several services. They bake breads with white flour; whole wheat flour; and now also a mix of different grains such as barley, amaranth, or quinoa. They bake small cakes, usually Brazilian sweet soda breads, and biscuits prepared with cassava starch called *biscoito de polvilho*. The starch has several names depending on the final product—it's called tapioca when preparing puddings, cakes, and pancakes. Called *polvilho* ("dust") when dry, it is used in the preparation of *brevidades* (small cakes), *pão de queijo* (cheese sticks), and similar small-sized biscuits and cakes. Bakeries also sell fresh fruit juices and coffee, and some serve lunch.

BUYING FOOD TODAY

The traditional *armazéns* (dry goods stores) were the place where families bought their weekly stocks of ingredients. They sold different kinds of beans; rice; olive oil; lard; flour; smoked, dried, and salted meats; and sugar, usually brown sugar. Old cookbooks had instructions on how to make a syrup and then clarify its impurities by mixing in egg whites. They used to have a notebook for writing down the goods that were to be picked up by family members. Payments were made biweekly or monthly. Richer families would send a list of items to the store once a week and the merchandise would be delivered later in the day. This retail system endured a long time in Rio. Each neighborhood had its own dry goods stores, which would have some crates with vegetables and fruits—onions, garlic, chayote, potatoes—just items to fulfill any occasional need.

Armazéns eventually also felt the passing of the time, and those that did not change to stores with self-service sets of shelves and freezers and cashiers at the door had to close. The older stores are long gone—Casas da Banha, Sendas, even Disco, which started in 1955 as a modern supermarket—replaced by Carrefour, Walmart, and Pão de Açúcar. But some smaller shops remain, especially in the southern part of the city. Zona Sul and Hortifruti sell an assortment of organic and fresh salads adequate for smaller families, and they have their own bakeries with more sophisticated goods. Throughout the city, there are also many local markets and regional food stores catering to various groups of consumers, as in Rio people from different parts of the country and from different social classes live in the same neighborhood.

Fine food retailing, as seen at the start of this chapter, was always subject to the arrival of a ship, to a law allowing their import, or some extraordinary circumstance, like the requisition by a captain of some caskets of wine. Fine foreign foods were for many centuries understood as goods of a higher quality, always better than the locally produced. Foreign cheeses, wines, chocolates, or canned goods, with the exception of the obvious extraordinary ones—caviar or foie gras—were consumed under special circumstances, and Christmas was one them.

Usually sold at shops that were also the importers and wholesalers, almonds, dried figs, walnuts, and chestnuts would arrive at Christmastime. These stores sold different sizes of wicker baskets full of delicacies. Their size would vary from small to very large ones, and they caused quite a stir when they arrived, especially as they usually were a gift sent from a friend or a client. The smaller-sized baskets might have a bottle of Port wine, one or two cans of Portuguese sardines or a liver pâté, one package of salted crackers, and one package of butter cookies, all artfully arranged with a ribbon tied around it. The larger ones to very large ones looked more like a wicker crate, with six bottles of wine, one Champaign, a jar or two with strawberry preserves, one with marmalade, French mustard, Spanish sausages, a jar with capers, and some even had a canned foie gras or cheeses. These baskets still can be ordered today, but, as most items can be bought in middle-sized cities or substituted by local high-quality goods, they have lost part of their enchantment.

Today many importers still endure with stores in older neighborhoods, mostly downtown. Sometimes new owners transform their buildings into restaurants or bars but keep their names, Casa Lidador is one of the last ones, and most of them specialize in selling wines, as the supermarket chains also have the same products with lower prices.

The best part of a food experience in Rio is that one can mix several centuries when buying items for a dinner. It is possible to make a phone call and order a traditional cake prepared with cassava and coconut from a family that bakes only this kind of cake. Fruit can be bought at an organic local market; fish can vary from the ubiquitous pink-colored salmon to a nice catch of the day from the fish market on the other side of the Bay of Guanabara. Green markets offer fresh, intense-colored vegetables, and there are ice creams, tropical fruit sorbets, and creative and healthy Popsickles, as well as French *pâtissiers*, Portuguese specialist in eggs creams, Italian pies, and Hungarian strudels. And of course, all the dishes prepared at home can vary according to taste and the age of the guests. Applets and websites are busily occupying the old niche of restaurant delivery, offering opportunities to discover new foods and online markets. The novelty of life online lies in the integration of several areas of the city, as the supplier does not have to be in any particular neighborhood as long as he offers products that consumers want.

Chapter Five

Restaurants and Eating Out in the City

The changes in the city after the end of slavery and the adoption of a republican government turned the country and Rio de Janeiro into an immigration destination. However, by the end of the 1920s, the nature of the city had changed from a small town to an ambitious international center, with casinos, restaurants, and bars.

Immigrants continued to arrive in search of new opportunities, and soon enough the provincial city had changed completely. Two decades before World War II, a more cosmopolitan population started to take over the existing public spaces of what was until then a relatively agrarian inland and to urbanize the beaches on the Atlantic coast. Today, a number of the restaurants from that time still survive, and their menus, although not exactly as they were, still carry dishes that are deeply ingrained in the food culture of the city.

TRADITIONAL RESTAURANTS

Rio de Janeiro's traditional restaurants are beloved by the population—some to the extent that if one of them moves to another address or closes because the owners retire, it causes a small commotion among its clientele. Sometimes, a group of friends, instead of surrendering to the owner's decision to close the bar, will even buy the business for the sake of indulging old habits.

These restaurants, and especially the bars—*botequims*—synthesize a certain ethos of the Carioca population. Cariocas see themselves as deeply ensconced in the local culture, and for them, eating and playing music, together if possible, is an important part of their identity. They are always looking for links in their everyday life that relate to the best aspects of their three most prominent original inheritances: the Amerindian, the African, and the Portuguese. Even those with ancestors from other places relate to this ethos.

Old traditional restaurants that establish a link to an earlier time of political importance or are perceived as representing a musical/artistic spirit are as important as the new, gourmet-oriented establishments. Actually, even those who prefer to patronize the modern new food places, with their creative and well-researched menus, also have a favorite traditional bistro, bar, or restaurant.

The traditional places can be separated into three categories by their food. There are the very traditional fish and seafood places, serving Brazilian-Portuguese food; the bistros, with large menus and more meat dishes than fish; and the traditional German-Brazilian restaurants, still going strong, with quite a large clientele! All these restaurants are very old, many starting business in the 1920s, and a couple of them more than one hundred years old. The oldest ones, with just about the same dishes they have always served, are Café Lamas, started in 1874; Rio Minho, 1884; and Bar Luiz, 1887.

In the traditional restaurants, the list of specialties includes large dishes like *feijoada*, which is black beans stewed with salted pork and jerked beef; codfish accompanied by spinach and cooked potatoes drizzled with olive oil seasoned with garlic; and octopus with broccoli and rice. Another specialty, *peixe à brasileira*, is fish fried in an egg batter, covered with a sauce made with tiny prawns cooked in a sauce of tomato and red and green peppers, with side dishes of rice and *pirão*, a typical cassava flour sauce. Rice prepared pilaf style is a standard side dish in these restaurants; there is no need to ask for it. Broccoli and spinach are frequently present, especially at lunch. Traditional restaurant menus feature complete meals, and rarely does one ask for a salad as a starter.

Most of these traditional restaurants are located in the old downtown, closer to the harbor or at Lapa neighborhood, near the aqueduct. In the 1920s, as the urbanization process really started to develop and change the Atlantic beaches, the neighborhoods became almost tourist resorts, with bars and restaurants offering some kind of regional food and beverages. There were few restaurants, mostly German establishments with their Alpine decoration or elegant restaurants with international cuisine. Later in the 1950s, children could eat a waffle or an ice cream at a coffee shop on the ground floor of Fred's, on Atlantic Avenue by the sea, but after sunset, Copacabana was all about cocktails at nightclubs like Vogue and Fred's with its spectacular shows. The city had more the spirit of a vacation resort than the capital of a country. Therein lies one of the secrets of Rio's admired lifestyle—this everyday balance of duty with leisure time.

Traditional restaurants have certain ways of serving their customers that always make them feel welcome. The rhythm is unhurried, and waiters usually know their clients and will bring them something to drink or chat a little as they

Young professionals pose for a picture around a table after a commemorative lunch, a common feature at the end of the year. *Source*: Courtesy of the estate of Professor Rosza Wigdorowicz vel Zoladz.

wait for a table. Some of the waiters have worked for a very long time in those establishments and are well known by more than one generation. The tables each have a white tablecloth and a small basket with bread, a saucer with olives, and rolls of butter, approximately one teaspoon for each person; some restaurants still offer toothpicks, even if etiquette manuals have banned them long ago.

Also in the traditional restaurant category are the old *cafés*. Quite a few have thrived since the 1920s, when they were places where politicians and bohemians could dine later in the night. They are in essence a marriage of a bistro, by the informality of the menu, and a bar, as many people go there to meet friends, drink *caipirinhas* and very cold beers, taste small savories, and eventually dine. Their menu listings usually offer vivid memories of the lifestyle in Rio from the time they started. Fish and seafood dishes are not their specialties, although one might want to ask for a grilled sea bass, and they serve a large number of combinations with shrimp and hearts of palm Bahia style—fried in oil and served seasoned with hot pepper sauce. As testimony to the passage of time, instead of rice served with shrimps, they now offer a risotto.

The dishes that made them famous, however, are steak and fries, shank of lamb, and old-fashioned beef scallops in Madeira wine sauce. They are the city's memories of food, and almost a timeline of preferences, as quite a few exemplify the decade they first appeared in the menus. The names of dishes are very Brazilian or of local reference: *tournedos*, a word previously used to describe the shape and thickness of the steaks, have completely disappeared from the menu of Café Lamas. Instead there is a "Metro Steak," possibly to honor the subway construction that dislodged the establishment from its original address, a historical place where even the presidents of the country would go to eat. If naming a recipe for such an incident appeared corny at the time, in the 1970s, today it adds a bit of character.

These restaurants, at least the ones that still resist the changes in the city, have wonderful names: Nova Capela—the original name was Capela but was changed when it moved to a new address—A Marisqueira, Adegão Português, Rio Minho.

Are they good? The food in these restaurants, because they are so old and patrons go there for their traditions, is the food that is expected. The reason people go to them is not their exceptionality, although sometimes one may hear that this or that place has a good cook at the moment. Rather, they represent a cultural moment, a place that recognizes itself as part of the Carioca culture, and where sometimes it is possible to eat very well.

A light fried fish with heart of palm and grilled plantain slices, Rio Minho restaurant at lunch hour, downtown Rio de Janeiro. *Source*: Marcia Zoladz.

POWER AND FOOD

The very old restaurants in downtown Rio, because they were geographically located close to the Brazilian government buildings, used to have among their patrons quite a few politicians, lawyers, journalists, and highly placed bureaucrats. Then as today, there was a tendency to favor some establishments over others. Power and constancy allowed these patrons to ask for their favorite dishes, even if not on the menu, or they would indicate special preferences or ask for adaptations. In appreciation, the dishes were eventually added to the menu with their creator's name.

One such dish is the *Filé à Oswaldo Aranha*, a steak covered with a hearty amount of fried garlic cloves, presented with a farofa and Portuguese fries— potato chips cut so thin they are almost transparent and fried until lightly golden and crunchy. They were the specialty of the two restaurants where Oswaldo Aranha, a diplomat and a minister of the Brazilian government, used to eat—Café Lamas and Cosmopolita.

Another dish is *Sopa Leão Velloso*, a fish and seafood soup. The story goes that Paulo Leão Velloso, a Brazilian diplomat, brought this recipe to one of the oldest restaurants in the city, possibly Rio Minho, during the 1920s, an adaptation of the bouillabaisse soup he ate in Marseille, France, and asked the chef to prepare it. Although there were several well-known personalities with this same family name in the city from the second half of the nineteenth century until the late 1920s, the official legend accepts the ambassador as the man who introduced the new recipe. Sopa Leão Velloso is, according to its recipe, a seafood and crustacean bisque. Like all bisques, first one makes a rich fish and seafood coulis and thickens it with a roux. Fish and seafood previously cooked in the fish broth are served together. It is delicious, easy to prepare, and has an easily recognizable French flair that was present in cookbooks from the late nineteenth and early twentieth centuries in Brazil. The true bouillabaisse, according to *Le Nouveau livre de cuisine*, however, is different.

The Brazilian *moqueca* or the Portuguese *caldeirada* are prepared in a similar way. It recommends stacking in a large pan several layers of fish, crayfish, langoustines, or any other seafood available together with one tomato; onions and garlic; olive oil seasoned with fresh herbs; salt and pepper; white wine; and a little saffron for color and just covering it with water. In ten to fifteen minutes the fish and crustaceans will be cooked. They are an accompaniment to the bouillon, served separately in deep dishes over bread slices.

MILK CUSTARD

The *pudim de leite* is a milk custard covered with a caramel sauce. Although served as a dessert in many restaurants, it is a typical homemade sweet, a variation of the Portuguese flan. An important part of the everyday meals of the city, the custard is much valued, despite the comment that follows every time it is served: "It's too sweet." Which is true.

The recipe today is usually prepared with sweetened condensed milk, allowing for little variation in its taste, although there is one recipe with grated Parmesan cheese in the batter and it is also possible to exchange part of the milk for orange juice. It became very popular in the 1950s when the first electric blenders became available in the country. As the recipe unites the ultimate act of modernity for young homemakers of that decade—opening a can—with the use of an electric device, it was an immediate success.

The only brand of sweetened condensed milk at the time—Milkmaid, or Leite Moça in Portuguese—was produced by Nestlé, and soon the custard was called "pudim de Leite Moça." After a couple of decades, the name changed back to milk custard. To prepare it, just beat all the ingredients together in a blender for one minute: one can of sweetened condensed milk and, using the can as a measure, two cans of whole milk and four eggs. Make a caramel with one cup sugar and half a cup water and transfer to a pudding form when golden brown. After the caramel sauce is completely cold, add the custard batter to the pudding form. Bake in a water bath, in a mild-to-hot oven

Pudim de leite e laranja, milk and orange custard covered with gold colored caramel, one of the favorite desserts of the cariocas. *Source:* Marcia Zoladz.

temperature for about one hour, or until the top is golden brown and the pudding still a little shaky. Let the pudding rest for one night in the refrigerator before removing it carefully from the form. It is extremely sweet.

Traditional Milk and Orange Custard

The traditional old-fashioned recipe is a little different, and especially creamy. It is rarely prepared nowadays, but worth the effort. Here is a recipe for a small flan.

1½ cups sugar for the caramel, plus ⅔ cup for the flan
1 cup milk
1 cup heavy cream
Peel of 3 oranges, grated
1 teaspoon pure vanilla extract
3 eggs
2 egg yolks

Cook 1½ cups of sugar on very low heat, constantly stirring, until the sugar has dissolved and acquired a light blond color. Transfer it to the bottom of a pudding pan. Turn the pan to coat the sides with the caramel. Heat the milk, the heavy cream, and the grated orange peels together, but do not let it boil; add the pure vanilla extract and turn off the heat source.

While the mixture cools, beat the eggs with the yolks and ⅔ cup of sugar until light colored and thick; blend in the milk and cream mixture. Transfer the flan batter to the pudding form and bake in a water bath for one hour. Test by inserting a toothpick or the blade of a knife in the batter close to side of the pan; it should come out quite dry. Leave the flan for at least six hours in the refrigerator after it has cooled down. Remove the flan very carefully from the baking form.

THE FIRST GERMAN RESTAURANTS DOWNTOWN AND BY THE BEACH

Starting a restaurant is one of the more common ways of finding work in a new country, and from the end of the nineteenth century when the urban immigration to Brazil started until the late 1920s, several German restaurants started to compete with the Brazilian-Portuguese and Spanish restaurants. They introduced new sausages, new seasonings—paprika, black mustard, fennel—sauerkraut, and veal, the famous Wiener schnitzel. They also opened new beer houses.

Their arrival coincided with an investment in the Atlantic beachfront of the city. First, a large hotel built at Copacabana Beach, the Copacabana Palace Hotel, was a project by Joseph Gire, the same architect whose Le Negresco opened in Nice, France, in 1923. All around this building grew an elegant neighborhood in the modern style of the 1920s, art deco.

Rio today, therefore, has a large cluster of upper-income art deco apartments by the sea, the majority of which are very well preserved by their owners. In order to keep their privileged view of the ocean they were built around a square called Lido. This open area today houses a school and several other establishments, but the buildings with their distinctive architecture are still there. Because both the hotel and the apartment buildings had the French Côte d'Azûr model in mind, most have shops and restaurants on their ground floor.

The bars and restaurants that today serve small fried savories then featured foreign specialties, especially German food, as it was quite a novelty to those visiting the beaches. They served sausages, and instead of the usual olive oil on the table, would have German-style mustards for extra seasoning. They are called black mustards in Portuguese, as opposed to the bright yellow mustard sauces. Their dark color is due to the brown mustard seeds and the dark sugar and apple or cider vinegar that were added for tanginess. Their duck with applesauce was quite well known, and on Sundays families would dine on large dishes with a selection of sausages, potato salad, and sauerkraut, with apple strudel for dessert.

German restaurants downtown had better luck than those by the sea. Many are still open for business today, catering to workers and students. They still have the same menus, with very simple and basic food—smoked *kassler* and *eisbein*. The owners also included very Brazilian steaks to their list of dishes, but with a German accent. The menu at *Bar Brasil*, one of the restaurants started in the 1920s, despite many concessions to its patrons, kept the ultra-Brazilian black beans stew off their list of dishes. Stewed lentils or white beans are served instead of the traditional black beans combination.

THE NEW ITALIANS

After World War II and into the 1960s, there were ten golden years when the city established a reputation as one of most charming places in the world. There were several reasons for this apparent exaggeration; first and foremost, the city had a young population, a famous beach—Copacabana—and warm weather, and it was far away from the consequences of the war Europeans were still confronting. No wonder so many young couples decided to restart their lives and raise their children in this place.

The city was the center of the communication industry, publishing eight daily newspapers and broadcasting very popular radio stations. With the many celebrities, artists, singers, and film stars coming to Rio, it was a welcoming environment for new restaurants.

There were two well-known Italian restaurants that introduced a new food genre in the city. Completely different from the city of São Paulo, where they had arrived in numbers large enough to influence the city lifestyle, Italians in Rio were very few, and came over just before or in the aftermath of World War II. Therefore, their alluring pastas and pizzas were unknown. These restaurants, with less conventional menus attracted young artists and others with late-night lifestyles. Leme, located at the edge of Copacabana Beach, was a bohemian neighborhood with plenty of artists, singers, and foreigners, people who loved to travel, and to eat. La Fiorentina and Cantina Sorrento, located close to each other, offered pizzas, pasta, and the ideal of a good life.

THE FRENCH BRIGADE

The city had to find a new vocation in order of continue its growth and create jobs after the government's move to the new capital, Brasilia, in 1960. One of the possibilities was to enlarge the activities around its most attractive beaches. At the same time, Copacabana Beach had to close the beach every year during the high tides, which interrupted traffic, and flooded several streets with salt water. The solution was a modernization of the shoreline; the sand strip was enlarged, broad sidewalks were redesigned, and hotels revamped or newly built. All this work of relocating the sand and building a new infrastructure took almost ten years, but with the help of the artist and landscape architect Roberto Burle Marx, the new landscape was ready in 1970.

The city has had a tradition of large parties with good French-Brazilian food served in beautiful hotels since the nineteenth century. In 1884, at the very elegant ballroom *Novo Cassino Fluminense*, the menu comprised six services in the salon and a buffet. There were fifty-six different entrées; desserts; dainty dishes like foie gras in aspic, turkey with truffles, grilled oysters, and *bijupirá* (*Rachycentron canadus*)—a large ocean fish presented with a tartar sauce. Twenty-two different drinks were available, including wines, champagne, liqueurs, dessert wines, orange juice, black and green tea, and German and British beer.

French restaurants were located downtown and in the south, close to the beaches of Ipanema, Leblon, and Copacabana. They were excellent places with French and Brazilian chefs, experts in elegance as well as the methods for cooking the traditional bourgeois dishes. Some were located in hotels,

A ballroom menu in 1878 offered fifty-six different dishes and desserts. *Source*: Courtesy of Fundação Biblioteca Nacional, Rio de Janeiro, http://objdigital.bn.br/acervo_digital/div_iconografia/icon1055667/icon1055667.pdf. Accessed December 11, 2015.

where they could cater to foreign guests, executives, and the local elite. The Copacabana Palace Hotel had a famous restaurant, O Bife de Ouro (The Golden Steak), where Hollywood stars would dine with local playboys. The restaurant at Hotel Ouro Verde, also on Atlantic Avenue, and Le Bec Fin, a restaurant in Copacabana, among others, allied good food with good service for the elites. They were elegant and expensive.

Besides remodeling Copacabana, the city prepared itself for new visitors, enlarging the importance of its annual Carnaval, turning it into the world-renown pageant. It was just then that the French nouvelle cuisine arrived in Rio de Janeiro, more precisely at the kitchens of the new Méridien Hotel, on Atlantic Avenue. This hotel had an enormous importance in the upgrading of the New Year's Eve festivities into a popular Réveillon party. Le Méridien immediately added a huge cascade of fireworks for New Year's Eve, and started to promote its new, young, and talented chefs at its restaurant, Le Saint-Honoré, working under a franchise of Paul Bocuse, one of the creators of the new interpretation of French traditional cuisine.

New Year's Eve was already a very popular festivity marrying two cultures. On one side, it is the Afro-Brazilian occasion of paying tribute to the mother of the sea with offerings of white flowers, perfumes, mirrors, and small feminine gifts as an expression of gratitude for her protection. On the other hand, there is the bourgeois commemoration of the date with champagne and a cold diner. The two festivities merged and turned into a popular festival that starts at dusk and ends with almost the whole population of the city dressed in white waiting for the sunrise.

With this new generation of young French chefs—the best known are Laurent Suaudeau and Claude Troisgros—the city awakened to new culinary possibilities, as they started to develop a French cuisine with Brazilian ingredients that today is just excellent food, without the need to explain itself. They literally changed the use of ingredients, bringing together Brazilian native ingredients with traditional cuts of meat in a way never done before. All of a sudden passion fruit was in a savory dish, rather than just used as juice or in ice creams and charlottes. They stripped the architecture of their restaurants of fusty details, and they were likewise straightforward with their food, each flavor easily recognizable and fresh. Their impeccable cuisine gathered a firm following in the city they embraced, with Laurent Suaudeau founding a school and Claude Troisgros launching popular TV shows.

A NOTE ON CARNAVAL

Carnaval is the festival that in Rio precedes the start of Lent, the forty days of penitence until Easter. During this time, the city explodes in a colorful and vivacious party, surrendering to music and dancing.

Officially, it starts on a Saturday and extends four and a half days, until noon on Ash Wednesday, the start of Lent in the Catholic Calendar. Mardi Gras, or Fat Tuesday, is one of the days of the festival calendar. On Ash Wednesday, the Christian calendar imposes its sobriety with the start of Lent, ending forty days later with Easter. The date, based on the lunar calendar, will vary from early February to middle March.

The festival in Rio is organized according to an official calendar based on a pageant, the parade of the schools of samba, which stops the city. The street parties start on Friday and only really end the next Saturday, when the winner of the pageant parades one last time. It officially ends the spirit of summer. There is no single special treat served in Brazilian bakeries, as one can find in Italy, for example, nor are there traditional dishes cooked only during Carnaval. Rather, as with many extended holidays, some families will gather for lunch around a traditional feijoada or eventually, if one is lucky, around a *cozido*, a broth prepared with dried and cured meats and several vegetables. Carnaval in the city starts early in the day, with music groups moving around certain neighborhoods, such as old downtown or Santa Teresa, a bohemian neighborhood located in one of the mountains where here are many bars and restaurants.

A Chinese folly at the top of one of the mountains offers one of the best views of the landscape, in 1911. *Source*: Wikimedia Commons, https://commons.wikimedia. org/wiki/File%3AVista_Chinesa_em_cart%C3%A3o_postal_de_1911.jpg. Accessed December 11, 2015.

A CHINESE FOLLY IN RIO: HOW TO EAT WITH CHOPSTICKS

High above the city, on the Serra da Carioca, on the way to the Tijuca Forest, it is possible to stop at a belvedere and take in the view. To the left the omnipresent statue of the Christ protects the city; looking down, the panoramic view of Guanabara Bay with its islands stretches for many miles. On the other side of the bay is the city of Niterói, and on clear days, the view stretches to the Serra dos Órgãos with the well-delineated profile of its highest mountain, Dedo de Deus, a mountain that indeed looks like God's finger pointing to the sky. Looking to the right, first there is the Lagoa Rodrigo de Freitas, the internal lagoon in the south of the city, and then the beaches of Ipanema and Leblon and the horizon. This landscape can be enjoyed from a structure built in 1903 to resemble a Chinese pagoda, an Art Nouveau building of concrete made to look like wood—very popular in its time, it was a reference to an earlier settlement of Chinese nationals in the region.

The first four Chinese arrived in Rio in 1811 to adapt tea plants in the country. Soon there were three hundred of their compatriots; they worked together with Portuguese botanists, but the tropical weather in Rio was not suitable for the plants, as they needed a different latitude and altitude to thrive. Also, their working conditions were similar to slavery, so they abandoned the endeavor. These first immigrants came from Guangzhou and arrived in groups until 1889, when the imperial government was replaced by a republic. At the start of the twentieth century, they started to arrive again, this time as small business owners, until the Japanese invasion of China in 1937 interrupted the immigration.

There were still other waves of Chinese immigration to the country related to political movements at home; many arrived after the Cultural Revolution in 1966. A small number of immigrants of Chinese origin moved to Brazil from Angola after that country's independence from Portugal and the start of the civil war in 1975. Their adaptation to Brazil was easier, as the Portuguese language is common to both countries.

The first immigrants started selling *pasteis* (fried dumplings) in the streets; from these they moved on to open restaurants—simple food such as sweet and sour pork or chop suey, but they were a novelty in Rio during the 1970s. The community thrived and expanded into more lucrative businesses, such as building and import/export, and their investments in Chinese restaurants waned. Today their children have university diplomas and a history of achievement in the country, and the Chinese fast food chains are not part of a their main businesses.

The beloved pasteis, part of the Chinese food heritage in the city, are large ones sold at the weekly green markets. The best way to describe them is a rectangular pouch of very thin dough, measuring approximately 15 × 10 centimeters (5 × 4 inches), fried in a vat of very hot oil; as the hot air inside the pouch expands and they puff, the dough gets crispy and acquires an attractive golden color. There is a choice of traditional fillings—often ground meat or chicken seasoned with a mix of onions, garlic, salt, pepper, and parsley. Another beloved filling is cream of hearts of palm—a béchamel sauce mixed with hearts of palm cut in small squares—or a square of mozzarella cheese. As a treat, one green olive is added to the filling. Local variations are always getting more creative too, such as pizza—cheese, tomato, and oregano—or cheese and banana. The amount of filling has to be very small in order to keep the dough pouches very light, allowing them to float in the oil vats. They are sometimes called *pasteis de vento*, wind dumplings, in a derogatory way, as the reason for the small amount of filling is not understood. But the aromas held inside play a big role in the experience of eating a fried pastel.

Another smaller kind of pastei, called *pasteizinhos*, are slightly different and not directly linked to the Chinese community. They have a larger amount of filling and are half-moon shaped, measuring around three centimeters. Their size makes them a good companion to a caipirinha or beer; whereas

the larger ones are more like a meal. Pasteizinhos are offered in bars and restaurants rather than as a street food, and they are more associated with local
gastronomy, filled with shrimps or with a cream of heart of palms, usually
served in small portions of six units at a time.

Pasteis could actually be dumplings of Portuguese origin, adapted by the
Chinese long ago and then again adapted to the local taste as they arrived
in Brazil. The Portuguese certainly learned from all the Asian cuisines
where they traded, starting in the sixteenth century, and they all have fried
pastries in the local food repertoire. They had a colony in Goa, India, from
1500 to 1961 and in Macau, in China, from 1557 to 1999; and in Japan,
they did not have a colony but introduced the first Catholic missions in
1549. There was also a colony in East Timor from the sixteenth century
until 1975.

The country of origin of the pasteizinhos is less clear than that of the large
pasteis; they can be vaguely associated more with a particular set of people
than a country. Within the Portuguese Empire, the same sailors, priests, and
officials went back and forth from Lisbon to Asia or moved to Africa and
Brazil, and they brought their own interpretations of the original Portuguese
cuisine. That is to say, they cooked their own style of locally influenced home
food, be it in India, China, Angola, Mozambique, or Portugal. It is in this fusion of unknown and various traditions that the origin of pasteizinhos may
be found. Lacking a specific foreign background, they are considered a local
food by the city inhabitants.

Pasteis Dough

The dough for large pasteis is sold at green market stalls, but it can also be
prepared at home. It will have the same taste as long as it is deep-fried in a
large pan.

3 cups wheat flour
1 tablespoon salt
2 tablespoons vegetable oil (canola, soy, or sunflower)
1 tablespoon *cachaça* (or other spirit, do not use rum)
1 cup warm water (more if needed)
Cornstarch for sprinkling the surface before spreading the dough
Oil enough for deep-frying the pasteis

Place flour and salt in the bowl of a mixer fitted with a kneading hook, start
the mixer and add the oil, the cachaça, and small amounts of water, until the
dough is very elastic and homogeneous.

Let the dough rest covered for half an hour, transfer to a surface slightly sprinkled with cornstarch. Work the dough with the hands lightly dusted with cornstarch, stretching and folding until it is soft and elastic. Press the dough several times through a pasta machine until very thin. The longer the dough sheets the more pasteis will be prepared at the same time.

Spread the dough sheets over a surface dusted with cornstarch. Cut several circles with three centimeters. Put one teaspoon of filling at the center of each half of a pastel, fold the other half over and using a fork press together and seal the three open sides. Fry the pasteis in approximately three inches of very hot oil.

WOULD YOU LIKE TO SURF?

In the early 1960s, a new sport arrived at Ipanema Beach, at Arpoador. Young men and a few girls ready to ride the waves on long boards would crowd the sea. They soon developed new tribal habits, rejecting the traditional rice and beans and introducing new ingredients, whole grains, and different breads also prepared with a greater variety of grains than the ones offered by the

A view of Ipanema Beach with the Morro Dois Irmãos. *Source*: Marcia Zoladz.

Brazilian-Portuguese bakeries. Their lifestyle models were the surfers living close to the sea in surf shacks in California and Hawaii.

No one had the habit of eating whole grain rice or whole wheat breads, although buckwheat and rye breads had been part of the German and East European tradition of the city. These new recipes featured soy sauce, the use of rye in desserts, cocoa powder without sugar added, a variety of Japanese chards instead of the usual green chard, and several recipes with tofu. It was an extraordinarily rich introduction to a new food vocabulary.

At first, there were small eateries, with communal tables, serving a large number of salads. Beans and alfalfa sprouts became a symbol for food that is healthy and full of positive bio-energy, despite their uninteresting taste, and jars of them began to be found in house and restaurant kitchens all over the area. There was a tremendous influence of the Indian kitchen, as surfers adopted yoga and Ayurveda. Some restaurants started to serve dishes based on Ayurvedic medicine; for example, soups prepared with lentils cooked in combination with other ingredients can be considered appeasing or stimulating. They also started the habit of drinking infusions as a refreshment, offering as a courtesy lemon grass, mint, or fennel freshly brewed in a thermos close to the cashier. Herbal infusions were offered to sick people for their healing powers and as a source of well-being.

By then a few surfers were trying the waters in Bali and India, and coming back with a large number of new ingredients such as green curry paste, and more sophisticated garam masala mixes, which added strong spices to the natural food restaurants. Meat, especially red meat, until then understood as part of the everyday diet, started to look quite menacing, being full of fat and laden with antibiotics, and it had to be avoided. On the other hand, most of the surfers were high school or college students with not much money, so their diet was healthy and suited to their youthful pockets.

Today these restaurants are part of the landscape, offering a more varied, more creative and contemporary menu, serving combinations of fresh ingredients in raw salads and braised mushrooms with slightly curried baked nuts and seeds, instead of beans, and instead of soy sprouts new baby arugula, or sweet-beet new greens are part of the composition.

The jump from a vegan or vegetarian diet toward a more colorful and apparently just as healthy food was quite fast. Japanese food arrived in Rio, again from California, completely adapted to a new and younger generation, although at first there were too many California rolls with their mix of cream cheese, mango, cucumber, and imitation crabmeat.

Japanese food with its colorful and healthy appeal arrived in full force and soon had the popularity of the fast food chains of the 1980s and took the place of the Chinese restaurants. As they also represented a good healthy food and offered a fun occasion for families, Cariocas soon learned to look for the restaurants that catered to the Japanese expatriates, which had a more authentic and varied menu.

The so-called natural food restaurants, *restaurantes naturais*, continued catering to a more select group that really lived in a vegan or vegetarian community. Their work is incredibly important, as they were the first to develop organic agriculture and to introduce new eating habits. They were able to show by pure neurotic insistence that breaking old rules in the kitchen is as important as keeping traditions. Moreover, they helped to develop and intensify the idea that a city with a healthy and athletic way of life, with a population swimming at its beaches, playing soccer, volleyball, and even badminton in its sands, has to pay attention to its food from farmer to market. As the 1990s approached, the city was ready to start a new cycle, with small charming restaurants run by young chefs. In Rio, there was a new generation of chefs arriving; instead of learning their profession at restaurants, they were college trained. These young men and women started new businesses with the stated purpose of offering new menus, but also of transforming the restaurant business in the city. They are the ones that compete with the multinational chains.

Surfboards at Prainha, one of several beaches in reservation areas in the west of the city. *Source*: Marcia Zoladz.

The first food chain in Rio, organized according to the North American business model, was Bob's, started in 1952 by an American-Brazilian tennis player, Bob Falkenburg. In the 1960s, the chain really had a very modern flair, with its large list of sandwiches, milk shakes, and soft ice creams. They had hot dogs and hot cheese and ham sandwiches and hamburgers. McDonald's only arrived in Rio in 1979, and its novelty was that they had a smaller menu based on hamburgers and its variations, fries, soft drinks, and soft ice creams and milk shakes.

At the start of the 1980s, a large number of shopping malls were built in the city, and they all have at least one floor with restaurants. It was the perfect opportunity for foreign chains to open establishments in the city, most of them already known to Brazilians, who had started to travel in large numbers to the United States, especially to Florida.

Today the city offers a huge variety of food styles in all its regions, from small restaurants where people eat instead of cooking at home to large *churrascarias*, serving the best beef raised under the care of dedicated farmers. There are restaurants serving French food of old and new cuisine, Japanese temakis prepared in an industrial kitchen or by Japan-trained chefs, and places serving fish and *bacalhau* in the middle of the forest or by the sea. There are varied interpretations of Italian food, and still there are the Chinese, the Spanish with their *cazuelas*, and the Germans from before and after World War II.

But the main type of restaurant or bar is the *boteco. Boteco* or *botequim* means "bar" or rather a shop that sells different sorts of beverages, cigarettes, and small appetizers. They have come a long way from their origin as dirty places full of drunks where one should not eat. Nowadays, each one has a specialty, mixing traditional ingredients such as jerked beef with molasses and hard cheese, shrimp encased in a pumpkin dough and fried, or plain fried fish served with a fresh mango sauce. They are the places to go in Rio to eat, have a beer, and talk to friends.

Chapter Six

Historic Cookbooks

How to Follow the History of the Recipes

Early Portuguese cookbooks mentioned in this chapter are those that had a direct influence on the way food in Rio was cooked, presented, or sold while Brazil was a province of Portugal from 1500 until 1822. Portuguese books were the ones known and possibly used by the colonial population. The first cookbook published in Portugal, in 1680, was *Arte da Cozinha* by Domingos Rodrigues.

Prior to this book, there are two known manuscripts with recipe collections. One is "Um Tratado da Cozinha Portuguesa do Século XV" (A Treatise of the Portuguese Cuisine in the Fifteenth Century), and the other "Livro de Cozinha da Infanta Dona Maria" (Cookbook of Princess Mary) with recipes from the first half of the sixteenth century. The *Infanta*'s notebooks were found in the National Library of Naples among a series of documents that were part of an archive of the Farnese family; it was possibly organized at the occasion of the marriage of the Portuguese princess with the then Duke of Farnese in 1565. This date it is quite helpful in order to understand what kind of food was available in Europe, for richer people.

Despite the infanta's name in the title, one cannot confirm that this powerful Renaissance princess, belonging to one of the richest countries of the time, was indeed eating these dishes. It is, however, a good guide to the ingredients and food-related habits of the nobility of the time, such as eating small birds or treating pies as part of the last dishes presented at dinners.

The recipes listed in the notebooks and in *Arte da Cozinha* include ingredients used in the Portuguese medieval kitchen, and at the same time, they are a good example of the Renaissance kitchen during the sixteenth century. The manuscripts of the Portuguese infanta, although found together in one binder, are in fact four smaller notebooks. Number one—*Manjares de carne*—is mostly pie recipes with meat, poultry, hare, and lampreys, the only fish listed in all four notebooks. Notebook number two—*Manjares de ovos*—has five recipes with eggs mixed with a little sugar and sprinkled with cinnamon in different proportions. Number three—*Manjares de leite*—has recipes that result in a cream, with eggs, a little sugar, and a little flour. Number four—*Cousas de conservas*—is about the preservation of foods. The recipes are for fruits preserved in sugar, what today we know as sweets such as marzipan, or almond brittle, and several fruit comfits. There is a recipe for candied orange peels, a pumpkin preserve, pears cooked in simple sugar syrup, and a *pessegada*—a peach cheese. It also has a mouthwash recipe supposed to be good for the gums; in the ingredient list are peppermint, honey, rosemary, pomegranate peel, salt, and a silver spoon of crushed pepper grains.

These first cookbooks also offer some hints about what was going on in Portuguese colonial kitchens—a vast world that started in Brazil passed through Africa and extended all the way to China, with a colonial outpost in Macao that had diplomatic and commercial relations with Japan. They made use of pumpkins from the Americas, cinnamon and pepper from India, and sugar from Madeira Island and Brazil.

The more one reads the recipes listed in Maria's notebook, the more a certain sobriety shows itself in them that is still recognizable in the kitchens of Rio. A good example is the very small amount of meat suggested, and the same recipe could be prepared with an alternative meat. There is a constant use of parsley and spring onions but no extra broths to season and add subtler and more complex flavors. These recipes do not suggest a large household kitchen with separate areas for different activities. Perhaps the intent of whoever gathered these recipes was to offer a small private Portuguese dinner to the infanta and her retinue.

By reading such old texts several possible analyses arise. The dishes in the manuscript indicate that it was important to keep a modest, as opposed to a gluttonous, household, at least in everyday life in an extremely religious country such as Portugal. *Galinha Mourisca* (Moorish chicken) is one recipe that has survived intact, exactly as written in the manuscript. The following translation retains all the word repetitions in order to maintain the didactic tone of the recipe. Six hundred years later it still does not need any extra help and can easily be prepared in a modern kitchen.

Galinha Mourisca—Take one whole chicken and cut it in pieces. Arrange the pieces in a pan with onions, parsley, salt, cilantro and mint, all greens, like for a salad, and two spoons of butter, a slice of lard, about the size of half an egg, all this in the pan with the chicken and all well covered with water. Cover everything well, as this is the only water used to cook the chicken. When almost ready, adjust the seasonings and add the juice of some lemons. After all is very well cooked, cut one bread in slices, put them on a dish, display the chicken pieces over them, arrange some cooked yolks over the chicken pieces and sprinkle with a little cinnamon.[1]

The manuscript of the Infanta makes one reference to Brazil, and although it is impossible to trace a direct relation to the local culture or to its popularity, it shows that whoever transcribed it around 1535 knew about its existence and about its sugar mills. The following translation is part of a recipe from the manuscript; it is for a very sweet and slightly fermented beverage. Later these kinds of beverages were called *aluás* and were prepared with pineapples. The recipe text does not recommend drinking it after five or more days, as it can cause drunkenness. The first documents about the distillation of the fermented juice of sugarcane, *cachaça*, started in the seventeenth century, at approximately the same time that British Caribbean colonies started producing rum.

> Sugar wine drunk in Brazil that is very healthy and wonderful for the liver
> In a large vase put six parts of fresh fountain water, two of them hot; the water should be warm. Add five pounds of good sugar, mix well, and cover. Let it rest in a warm place; boil it once or twice. After one day it is ready to drink, and it is very good.[2]

One hundred years later, the following mutton meatballs recipe is one of many basic examples from the *Arte da Cozinha*; by then a no-nonsense use of ingredients was already a characteristic trait of Portuguese gastronomy, still without tomatoes in its sauce, but with a generous amount of fresh herbs. The text shows a well-formed culinary vocabulary and cooking method that expanded toward a more complete local cuisine and offers a glimpse into the typical homemade food of the late seventeenth century. Tomatoes would be included later in the lists of ingredients.

This is in fact a small-portioned recipe for one or two persons and uses the rest of a leg of mutton. It is difficult to know in retrospect why a recipe makes the list in a cookbook. The *Arte da Cozinha* was a kitchen guide for larger houses; there are, however, recipes with smaller amounts of ingredients that suggest this food was prepared for the elderly or the children in a rich kitchen.

The original measurement used was called in Portuguese *arrátel*, it was part of a weight system used in scales in Portugal since early in the Middle Ages; it equaled a pound, or 16 ounces, during the Renaissance.

> Mutton meatballs: Two pounds of cleaned mutton leg cut in very small pieces, mixed with one quarter of lard mixed with seasonings. Add three yolks, soft crumbs of one bread, parsley and other fresh herbs, some vinegar and salt. Make the meatballs the size you want, adjust the seasoning and cook them in water. Thicken the sauce in the pan with three yolks. Arrange the meatballs in

individual portions over a slice of bread spread with fresh butter; cover them with their sauce and season with a little juice of lemon and a pinch of cinnamon.[3]

There are several recipes from the infanta's manuscript and from early Portuguese cookbooks that have survived in Portugal as part of the culinary culture and can stil be found not only there but also in Brazil. Maria de Lourdes Modesto, a Portuguese cookbook author, gathered all these recipes in *Cozinha tradicional portuguesa*.[4] They are separated by region, including Madeira and the Azores Islands. The richness and coherence of the recipe repertoire put together by the author is so vast that it also serves as a testimony and annotation on Portuguese food.

The early cookbooks are a constant reminder of the origins of the method of cooking in Rio until today. The basic list of seasonings used in everyday food recipes is still here. They start with a recommendation to brown an onion until lightly colored together with one or two garlic cloves. More often than not in early times lard was the favored fat, or the only one available. There is no tradition of using goose fat, but imported olive oil; it was called sweet oil—*azeite doce*. Although not all olive oils leave a sweet after taste, in the seventeenth century it was considered sweet in contrast with the salt in the lard or butter, often with a rancid taste. The next step is to include some fresh seasonings and the meat or vegetables to be prepared.

Sweets are another proud inheritance from the Portuguese that survives in Rio and is also well documented in cookbooks both in Brazil and in Portugal. They are usually considered a monastery tradition, even when not all were prepared by religious orders. Elegant or more elaborate desserts and sweets for special occasions today in Rio are ordered at small catering services in which a whole family is usually employed.

Some families specialized in specific cakes; they could be made with dozens of eggs for instance. Others baked petit-fours, or small sweets prepared usually by assembling a dried fruit and a cream; the favorite flavor might be vanilla or coconut, all encased in hard transparent caramel.

The tradition began very early in Portugal during the Middle Ages when in order to enlarge their revenues monastic orders and households started to manufacture sweets and fruit pastes and preserved fruits in sugar syrup made from sugar cane, introduced in the Iberian Peninsula by the Arabs. Each city has its traditional regional sweets. For example, Aveiro has the *ovos moles*—a cream prepared with egg yolks and sugar syrup. In Brazil, a small amount of coconut milk is mixed in the sugar-and-yolks cream and is called *baba de moça* (maiden's dribble). The name of this recipe together with a few others in the Portuguese sweets repertoire, such as *barriga de freira* (nun's belly) and *papos de anjo* (angel's neck), have sensuous overtones, possibly a reference to their soft texture.

By 1788, traditional sweets were already part of the Portuguese taste, and the third cookbook published in Portugal was *Arte nova, e curiosa para conserveiros*, a manual on the art of preparing a large variety of sweets. Again, like the older Portuguese cookbooks, the text has very detailed explanations, easy to follow for an apprentice to use as a reference for recipes. The amounts of sugar suggested in the recipes are, even for today's Brazilian standards, very generous, suggesting that the size of the sweets served to each person may have been very small. The portions were more like tastings, a little restorative placed in a dish at the table, rather than as a centerpiece cut in generous slices and shared as in a contemporary dessert.

BOOKS IN BRAZIL

The Portuguese practice of preparing and selling sweets was also common in Brazil during colonial times, especially in Rio with its lively street market. Poor widows, monasteries, and cloisters who led lives completely closed off from the public eye would have at least one employee taking orders or selling their sweets on the streets, as nuns and women did not go out of their houses except in a procession to commemorate their saints of devotion or on their way to visit relatives. Women could only go out accompanied by a son, a husband, or at least a male slave; they rarely left their houses by themselves.

Like everything else in Carioca culture, the sweets and the fruit paste recipes more often than not are reinterpreted for a less elitist culture. The colonial kitchen was the place where tradition was reinvented and where food acquired a completely new use. A good example is the *casadinho* (meaning roughly "sweetly married"), which is two cookies joined together with guava paste or milk marmalade that can be bought at street markets. It is an informal version of the *bem-casado* ("well married"), two small rounds of *genoise* cake attached by a thin layer of cream of eggs, or nowadays, the preferred, although not so elegant, milk marmalade, all bathed in a sugar syrup, and wrapped in beautiful paper, tied with satin and velvet ribbons. They are presented in heavily worked silver trays as a take-away gift at weddings; their meaning, like confetti, is to wish a sweet life to the new couple.

During the second half of the nineteenth century, shortly after the independence from Portugal in 1822, while the national identities were surfacing and those born in the country began to see themselves not just as Portuguese who had remained in an ex-colony, cookbooks began to add local dishes to their recipe list. These cookbooks, written in Rio had a mix of Portuguese and French food in their recipe lists.

The first one, *O cozinheiro imperial*, published in 1840, has a list of recipes that did not take special regional ingredients into account; rather, it is a portrait of what was eaten and available in Rio de Janeiro and in the rural area surrounding it. Even if it is not possible to affirm who the intended readership of this book was, the recipes were not for foods prepared in the kitchens of private households.

What makes this book particularly valuable is what the recipes tell us about the dishes prepared at restaurants, public houses, and at supply services for the harbor of Rio and for the military. Although they do not list the amounts needed together with the ingredients, an experienced cook would prepare large amounts according to the day's or week's menu.

The first chapter, "Soups," teaches how to make different broths to be used in soups and in sauces, such as broth prepared with beef and poultry meat cooked together and "general and ordinary broth"—a simple broth prepared only with the legs. They include very elegant broths as well, easily transformed into sauces for veal, poultry, beef, and fish. This chapter includes fourteen broths for different ailments, colds, and hangovers, such as a chicory broth, a light broth for the sick, prepared with chicken and veal. The book also has a very good recipe for preparing beef boullion cubes that could be stored for a very long duration.

The Portuguese food repertoire is still very strong in its pages, despite its very pretentious name (Brazil was an empire with only one colony, Uruguay, from 1821 to 1828), and it ignored the country's independence from Portugal in 1822. Contrary to the popular view that offal was the kind of meat left over for servants and slaves, there are several recipes for it. Everybody happily consumed livers, kidney, tails, and all the entrails.

Servants and slaves on farms did not have the chance to eat meat at all, as their daily rations were rice and beans; whatever extra they ate was obtained in small garden plots they were allowed to tend. In the cities and especially in richer houses there was a separate food for household personnel, but they usually ate lunch and dinner prepared with the day's leftovers and from other lunches and dinners. This was what the middle classes and lower classes also ate. Leftovers were inevitable—so small portions of rice and green beans would be mixed with an egg and some extra salt and pepper, molded into small patties, and fried; leftover meat would be shredded, mixed with bread crumbs, and fried.

The second book, *Cozinheiro nacional*, with savory dishes, published sometime between 1860 and 1870, and its partner *Doceiro nacional*, with desserts and sweets recipes, together offer a good appraisal of what was eaten in many households; some were indeed on its tables until late in the twentieth century. They inlude recipes for small- and medium-size animals such as agouti (*Agouti paca*); pigeons and small birds caught in the surrounding woods; and large, heavy-tailed lizards and turtles caught with nets. There are six recipes for armadillo; luckily, they explain how to choose the best ones, making one wonder how often a cookbook reader would have the opportunity to prepare them. Even if it is a little difficult to know how often these Brazilian animals were cooked in the city, they certainly were in more rural areas in or around town, so it is understandable that such recipes should be included in a national cookbook.

There is in these books a list of the ingredients that, short of starving, nobody would eat nowadays, and somehow they have a colonial and too exotic touch. A good example is a recipe for parrots in rice. Parrots were always beloved house pets, and the image of the Brazilian bourgeoisie eating them seems questionable by the simple fact that no one eats their own pets. Perhaps they did. But parrots in the one hundred forty-five years since the book was published have long moved from the category of food to that of house pet, and from there moved once again to protected wild animal status.

Other suggested recipes are delicious. One can read how to cook black beans, make calf foot's jelly, and find the best filling for codfish quiche in *Cozinheiro nacional*. The *Doceira brasileira*, its contemporary, has a list of desserts and sweets that are still part of the table of quite a few households, especially because they are so common that they can be bought in stores today. Coconut flummery, dried fruits, fruits swimming in a caramel sauce spiced with cinnamon and clove, braised duck with quinces—just saying the recipe names aloud makes them sound delicious, but they are not especially from Rio.

The noteworthy word in the books' titles is *national*, confirming the willingness of the author to place Brazilian cuisine in an enlarged context at that moment; from the country's point of view, it meant a place alongside European recipes. Some of them offer a combination of French and local food, for example, omelets with *piabas*, a small freshwater fish of Brazil.

Questions of etiquette were in high demand if one is to judge by all the information on how to set a table, how to present dishes, and how to trim down a menu was indeed necessary. The *cozinheiro imperial* was the first cookbook published in the newly independent country. There was, however, no denying that the city was far from the fashion centers and quite provincial in comparison to Paris or London, and it aspired to change. There was a constant recommendation in all books to "improve" the food sequence at meals in Brazil, and especially in Rio, where the government and all the embassies were located.

Social life was kept closeted inside Brazilian families; there were no public social gatherings as in bourgeois life in England, for example. Even if there were balls and parties for the younger generation, they were always at the house of a family member. The imperial family was not very gregarious and would rarely promote such large gatherings.

Reading these books from the first half of the nineteenth century, and in fact reading Brazilian cookbooks from a century later, they all have after the introduction or at the end menu suggestions for different occasions and diagrams of the best way to seat your guests and organize all the service— cutlery, plates, glasses, napkins, and so on. Apparently, until the middle of the nineteenth century there was still the rural local habit of presenting several sorts of meat together with vegetables, beans, and pastries at the same time. Otherwise, there would have been no need to recommend a more orderly sequence, as in the introduction of the first edition of the *Cozinheiro imperial*. Ten years later there is still a very generous lists of dishes to be served for lunch in *Cozinheiro nacional*, already written in the typical Portuguese language of the city—affectionate with plenty of diminutives—and the recipe list can be found today in many traditional old-style restaurants, but not at homes. It is a large amount of food, but what a colorful table! Who would not like to be invited to such a lunch! The custom of serving at parties a varied number of dishes together, without a regular sequence is still part of the eating habits of Brazilian families. It has the same implication as a banquet in the Renaissance—presenting the family to its best advantage with an appetizing choice of dishes, but in an appropriate size.

LUNCHES FOR SIX OR EIGHT PEOPLE

At the center of the table, display a sirloin à la *française* with the sauce prepared by a good cook.

One cruet each with salt, pepper, vinegar, mustard, and olive oil.

Four little cold dishes: one with fresh butter, one with radishes, one with sardines prepared in Nantes way, and one with washed olives.

Four little hot dishes: one with calf's feet filled, one with pork ears with its pulp, one with braised chicken breast, one of frog legs.

Two hot entrées: sweetbreads en *gelée*, one baked chicken with cream.

Dessert: One pie made with *requeijão*; one shrimp quiche; one London cheese; one Dutch cheese or a cheese from Minas Gerais; one dish of dried sweetmeats; there were usually fruits cooked in sugar syrup, dried in the sun, and covered in sugar; it could be green figs, green peaches or pears, quinces, papayas, or pineapples.

A Note on Brazilian Cheeses Cited in This Menu

Close to Rio de Janeiro, the Province of Minas Gerais was and still is a large dairy production center. Besides all the large industrially produced types of cheeses, the region today produces two very appreciated regional cheeses, each with several local variations. There is a fresh cheese called Minas, with half-cured and hard variations, prepared with raw milk and with exquisite flavors. Traditionally, one serves cheeses as a complement to fruit pastes and fruit compotes, and as a dessert. There is also a beloved soft cheese, *requeijão*, a creamed cheese prepared by cooking the milk curd until it has a tender and uniform texture. Slightly salted it is also served with guava paste for dessert or for breakfast.

Several Portuguese cheeses were imported throughout colonial times from Portugal, *queijo do reino*—cheeses from the kingdom. Their texture and flavor was similar to the Dutch cheese Edam or a young Cheddar, with a strong yellow coloring and a sharp aftertaste in the mouth; they are the origin of quite a large line of Brazilian cheeses. The Minas cheese started local production in the eighteenth century and has its origin in the fresh cheeses made with sheep's milk in the Serra da Estrela in northern Portugal, only in Brazil they use cow's milk.

AFRO-BRAZILIAN INFLUENCE

What the books also tell in their recipe lists is that cooks in hotels and private homes in the second half of the nineteenth century were building an intercultural food exchange, introducing typically African ingredients into urban households—yams, okra, a large number of local vegetables, and roots colored with the red food coloring annatto. Most cooks were of African origin—free and slave—from both sexes, but in homes the majority were women.

They also brought changes to the desserts in Rio. Typical Portuguese desserts acquired a richer texture and a deeper flavor with shredded coconut or coconut milk, and local and imported tropical fruits entered the recipe lists without any comment as to their exotic origins. In the nineteenth century there was a large migration from Africa to Rio de Janeiro, as the sugar industry in the northeast declined and coffee farms in the southeast close to the city—and even in the city—produced a more valuable commodity.

It is from this period that a Brazilian-African kitchen in Rio began using peppers, palm oil, and dried shrimps as seasoning or as an emulsifier, creating a different flavor. It was the kind of food served at lunch for workers as well as travelers and foreigners living in small hotels around the city. One hundred years later, the dishes prepared with these ingredients are part of the commemorative food usually served on birthdays, Christmas Eve, or special dinners. The perfectly balanced food of Portuguese origin, with its large number of vegetables, eggs, fish, and pork, achieved a Brazilian identity, and in Rio this rich fare was further reworked to bring out more subtle flavors.

SWEET STATEMENTS IN THE KITCHEN

In Brazilian culture it quite usual to give names to sweets, cakes, muffins, and cookies. Sometimes they are dedicated to love, as in *Amor aos pedaços* (pieces of love), a cake with pineapple. There are still those named after saints, many with origins in Portuguese monasteries, such as the Santa Clara pastries, small pies prepared with filo dough filled with cream of eggs, or Saint Anthony's cake, a light peanut genoise batter. In Brazilian-Portuguese folk culture Saint Anthony is considered capable of helping young women find a good husband.

There were, however, two very important moments reflected in the kitchen. First there was the independence from Portugal in 1822, when for the first time sweets were named in honor of its new status, *Doce do Brasil* and *Brasileiras* were dainty sweets that may have their origins around this time or even earlier. The former is a corn cream, and its name rather confirms its geographical origin, the best description is a crème brulée prepared with very tender sweet corn grains, mashed, sifted, cooked in a sugar caramel and again baked until gold colored in the oven. *Brasileiras* were little balls of two and a half to three centimeters made with egg, sugar, and grated coconut and baked until a little dried and slightly scorched on the outside but still moist on the inside. Both recipes still exist today, but their names have not survived, as there is no need to assert a national origin independent from the colonial masters. Both recipes are in the oldest Brazilian dessert book, *Doceira brasileira*.

However, two political events at the end of the nineteenth century and the turn of the century in itself had a strong impact in the population. The first event was the end of slavery in 1888. Abolitionist movements had started some years earlier, with newspapers, lawyers, and Parliament representatives from different states in support. At this same time there was discussion and conflict around the second major political event: the moment for the empire had ended. It was time for Brazil to get into the modern political world, as the other countries in the Americas had done, with a Republican government.

Why did the recipes of this time receive celebratory names as if they were a political commentary? It is hard to answer this question without a contemporary testimony. There is an imperial cake, an end-of-the-century cake, and a republican pudding recipe in the Brazilian repertoire. They appear in some books and in notebooks. All are very simple recipes: a Portuguese-style cake with a large number of eggs, an angel food cake, and a flan.

Imperial Cake

The recipe is quite easy to prepare, despite the large number of eggs. The only contemporary recommendation would be to add a teaspoon of baking powder to guarantee the cake will rise to the right height.

400 g butter
2 cups sugar
14 eggs, separated
2 cups wheat or rice flour
1 teaspoon baking powder (optional)

Beat the butter with the sugar until light and fluffy. Beat the egg whites very well, and add the yolks. Beat a little longer. Add the egg mixture to the butter and sugar mix, alternating with the flour. Pour batter into a greased and floured rectangular baking dish. Bake until lightly golden. Dust with sugar, and cut the cake in squares or diagonally.
(Recipe from the notebook of M.M.A. from 1906.)

Bolo Fim de século

This "end-of-the-century" cake recipe uses a genoise batter prepared with egg whites, an angel food cake, quite unusual in Brazil, where the bright color of the yolks are favored in desserts. The texture is quite delicate, however a little dry. Possibly a little fruit preserve or marmalade would have been at the side in a beautiful crystal cup, as a complement. The name and recipe suggests it was a teacake served on special occasions.

4 egg whites
4 soupspoons (tablespoons) of sugar
4 soupspoons plain flour
1 coffee spoon (a little less than a teaspoon) baking soda
1 soupspoon butter

Beat the egg whites until they form soft peaks, add the sugar, one spoon at a time, and keep on beating until the meringue is thick, smooth, and shiny. Mix the flour with the baking soda and sift over the egg whites. At last, fold in the melted and almost cooled butter. Bake in a grease and floured baking form.
(Recipe from the notebook of M.M.A.,1906.)

Republican Pudding

600 g (3 cups) sugar
150 g (5 oz) flour
½ teaspoon grated nutmeg
12 egg yolks
6 whites
1 liter (1 quart) milk

6 glasses of Port wine (old recipes used the appropriate glass as measurement, their sizes would vary according to the serving etiquette. The same rule would apply to liqueurs or sweet wines used in pies, cakes, or cookies batters).

Sugar for the caramel sauce

Mix the sugar, the flour, and the nutmeg. Add one by one the egg yolks and the whites, without stopping to beat. Then mix in the milk and the wine. Make sure the flour does not settle at the bottom.

Cover bottom and sides of a pudding form with a thick caramel, add the pudding batter and bake in a water bath until done.[5]

(Note: the original recipe asks for half a grated nutmeg; I have trimmed it for modern tastes.)

An Instant in the Life of a City—Silvia's Cake

Recipes were indeed a communication form, and sometimes through them, one is allowed a glimpse of the life in a city, especially inside the private lives of the population. At the turn of the century in Rio one cake started to appear with a certain frequency in notebooks and in recipe books as well. The name of the recipe is Silvia's Cake.

The big surprise is how this cake became Silvia's Cake, with its name written in English in Brazilian recipe notebooks. If we analyze the following recipe, we find a flat cake with grated almonds in the dough and an orange icing. The quantity of sugar, in relation to the other ingredients, is not different from that recommended for cakes baked in the old homes in a culture of plenty and cheap sugar. The result is a cake quite different from those produced in the old farm kitchens. Smaller, with a more urbane appearance, it could be called elegant; it does not use ingredients of markedly colonial origin—fewer eggs, no manioc or cassava paste (*puba*) and no corn flour. Moreover, it has a sugar and orange juice frosting that plain cakes usually do not have. The cake reflects a change in Brazilian life. Its name probably did not have to be written in English in the notebooks, but then it would not have had the same cultural significance. This was a recipe for young people.

The recipe for Sylvia's Cake may vary a little, but it always uses the same measure of flour, sugar, and butter. The number of eggs may differ, either five or four units, the text lists the ingredients and assumes the reader knows how to make a cake.

250 grams butter, 250 grams sugar, 250 grams flour, four whole eggs, two yolks, one saucer whole almonds, and then ground. Cream the butter, add the sugar and beat well, then the eggs, the flour and, lastly, the grinded almonds.

Bake in baking sheet lined with parchment paper. Regular heat. Frosting: 200 grams sugar, juice from two oranges, and the "sap" of one more (obtained by grating the peel of an orange, mixing it with its juice and then straining the result). Cover the cake with this frosting as soon as it comes out of the oven. Let it cool, cut in small diagonal pieces.[6]

The reason why Silvia's Cake had such a good reception was that it was more than a simple almond sponge cake. Its name being in English represented modern times in a rural country with slavery still a living memory. A "cake" (written in English) brings to mind a very different vision of the future than an afternoon corn cake or a manioc pudding—even one that has a delicate taste and is soft and sensual to the bite. The fascination is entirely in the name and very little in the recipe of an almond cake in a culture filled with almond cake recipes. However, in Brazil we made a concession: to the cream of eggs, known in Portugal as *ovos moles* (floppy eggs), was added coconut milk—*baba de moça*, and this is a sauce still served today with the almond cake.

Why have we stopped baking the Silvia's Cake and all other almond cakes? What changes happened in the life of Brazilians to make all such cakes with almonds or walnuts no longer a symbol of refinement? The question is indeed metaphoric. The answer lies in the industrialization that was at first understood as the arrival of progress and in the introduction of smaller gas stoves that completely changed baking habits at the turn of the nineteenth century.

The Société Anonyme du Gaz, a fuel company since the nineteenth century in the city, created cooking schools to stimulate the use of the new stoves, and published off and on, one has to admit, a series of culinary arts books. Mostly they had a large number recipes, sometimes with more than one thousand, as in *Arte Culinaria Brasileira*, which was quite impressive. The authors introduced themselves as part of the school system of the company.

Little by little, a new cake took over the position of best cake in the world—the chocolate cake. In Brazil at the beginning of the twentieth century, these recipes still appear in notebooks and books without baking powder, brownie-style, or French chocolate cakes, quite low, instead of the later more appreciated ones with many layers. In Brazil the chocolate cake only becomes synonymous with a good cake after World War II.

FOOD IN A BELLE ÉPOQUE MOOD AND SOME EARLIER POLITICAL STATEMENTS IN THE KITCHEN

Right before and after the end of World War I a large number of immigrants were responsible for the growth of the the editorial market in Brazil. There were more readers, and cookboks also started to be more frequently published.

There were two kinds of cookbooks. One of them was the professional manuals for either household or restaurant employees, one of the best known and longer lived was *O Cozinheiro Popular*, which included recipes and training advice for cooks, bakers, and pastry chefs. Quite a few of the instructions today are useless, aligned with a turn-of-the-century interest in the exaggerated use of specialized cutlery and service dishes for every occasion. The second kind was the books published for households, where young ladies would read them with their mothers and grandmothers, especially in preparation for parties, when new dishes were tested and served along with the favorites of the family.

These books may have a large list of recipes or a perhaps whole chapter with different egg recipes. They tell readers that eggs deserve a better presentation in dainty and delicate silver carriers, they teach to poach eggs in a special pan with a small ladle-like support for each one. Old families today, as a rather idiosyncratic tribute to a long lost time, still poach eggs in a ladle, a quite practical leftover technique for cooking just one unit, with the raw egg inside the ladle submerged in boiling water until the white turns opaque. Having so many pages dedicated to eggs makes their preparation acquire a symbolic value.

Eggs in these books are an urban meal, contradicting the rural image of several chicken nests spread around the backyard with children chasing for them and poking at the poor chicken to see how many eggs were there. This is a change started at elegant hotels in spa and seaside towns in Europe serving *Oeufs en gelée* or with Mornay sauce, but it soon arrived in Rio in the shape of small soufflés; cookbooks at the time had a large number of recipes with eggs as its main ingredient. The upgrade of this very simple rural ingredient did not happen only in Rio, *Le nouveau livre de cuisine*, a French cookbook, dedicated thirty-six recipes to eggs alone, maybe these recipes should be considered witnesses of urban change.

Especially omelets deserve a certain attention in these early books, as they are easy to prepare, and a single one goes a long way, feeding two people, and their presentation, delicately folded, also allows chefs and home cooks to exert a serious approach to cooking on a very limited budget. Who can deny the perfection of an omelet made with fresh eggs, almost cooked—*baveuse*, as the French call it?

TOWARD THE FUTURE: BOOKS FOR A MODERN CITY

Alegria de Cozinhar (*Delight in Cooking*) was published as a gorgeous all-around cookbook in 1954—cuisine bourgeoise with a new look for young and urban homemakers. It had more of the same kind of very conservative recipes, only with a new language. The new woman should serve a more informal lunch—usually rice with black beans, a vegetable, and either fish or meat; and for dinner a fish or soup to start, a meat or poultry dish including rice, and dessert. The 718 pages were filled with recipes, notions of etiquette, and recommendations for setting a table, but there was not a real change from the books published in the nineteenth century.

This book and a couple of other ones that taught women how to cook everything in the Brazilian repertoire had the best recipes one could wish for, except for the fact that they were published with the intent of repeating the old ways. They assumed a household with a conservative structure—sometimes comprising more than just the husband, wife, and children. It was quite commmon for a widowed aunt or a grandmother to live with the family, and until the 1960s, quite a few families, even middle-class ones, kept their older and retired nannies at their homes. Therefore, these texts assumed more than one woman living in the same house with lots of time on their hands after lunch time to prepare pies, fruit ice creams, and very light arrowroot biscuits called *sequilhos*.

Sequilhos

One pound arrowroot—half a pound sugar—2 tablespoons milk—4 tablespoons butter—1 egg—a pinch of salt.
    Knead all ingredients together, make the biscuits, arrange them on a lightly greased baking sheet and bake them in a hot oven. The sequilhos bake quickly. They should stay almost white, the color of the arrowroot.[7]

Receitas Culinárias, written by Myrtes Paranhos in 1962, was the first book for the new times in the city, having a bossa nova mood, with recipes from a restaurant and not for the traditional homemaker. It was the first, at least in Brazil, to have the recipes of a restaurant not because of its food but because of the celebrities that dined there. Paranhos was the owner of a small bistro called, very appropriately, Le Petit Trou, a place where actors and singers used to check in after their performances. The recipe names were dedicated to her clientele and made this book completely true to her restaurant concept. And nothing could be closer to the French bistro, a neighborhood place with good food where the owner is always hanging around. At this point, food in Rio completed an evolution that defined what it was and what it is today, completely integrated with the spirit of the city—a difficult place for pompous high gastronomy but welcoming for very good and creative food, always informal.

Cookbooks from the 1970s onward concurred with the magazine and newspaper industry, which had a broader reach, especially women's and teenagers' magazines. A women's magazine featured a larger number of subjects, offering the reader updates on more than just recipes. They explained to Brazilian women such important issues as women's rights, divorce, and how to raise their daughters differently from how they had been raised by their mothers. The largest magazines were *Claudia*, published by Editora Abril, and *Desfile*, published by Editora Manchete, which closed after the death of its founder.

Also at the same time another kind of magazine reached the newsstands—the weekly or biweekly collectible, which featured many cooking issues; after six months or a year, a completed series could be bound with a hard cover that was also sold at newsstands. Subjects varied from Brazilian regional food to cooking classes to general interest, such as children or parties or wedding cakes.

Rio was not different from other cities with the growth of large TV networks interested in developing local contemporary shows with young chefs. At the end of the 1990s, a new generation of chefs, more open to showing their works in different media, was coming of age with new recipes and international training. The pioneers in this type of cooking were Flávia Quaresma from Rio and Alex Atalla from São Paulo; they also had one of the earlier modern shows *Mesa para dois* (Table for two), on the GNT cable channel in 2005. Focusing on a new ingredient or a new place they visited, each show taught viewers about restaurant cooking techniques that could be used at home.

Recipe cookbooks in Brazil today are part of the global communication industry; chefs have their own shows in large television networks, with cookbooks and websites and social networks working together to publicize their work. Celebrity chefs from around the world with shows on international networks also reach Brazil, have their books translated, and are as successful in Rio as in their home countries. There are also several local equally important chefs with their own shows; one of the more successful chef's in Rio, who besides having his own restaurants, has a very popular TV show, is the Frenchman Claude Troigros. With *Que marravilha* he achieved a tremendous popularity preparing local food with a French accent.

Besides those exhibiting the work of chefs, there are also new shows in Brazil demonstrating to a broader audience the flavors of regional specialties cooked either in Rio or around the country. These shows reflect a new curiosity and a Brazilian food repertoire for a newer generation of chefs looking to experiment with well-known ingredients in a new way. New chefs in Rio today are working together with photographers, anthropologists, agronomists, and farmers, striving to grab what is local and blend it with their own individual tastes.

Notes

CHAPTER ONE

1. SOS Mata Atlântica, acessed January 27, 2016, https://goo.gl/shVfEO
2. Fernão Cardim, *Tratados da gente e terra do Brasil*, edited by Ana Maria de Azevedo (São Paulo: Hedra, 2009), 127. Cardim was a Jesuit priest who lived for two long periods in Brazil from 1583 until 1625.
3. Maria Cecília Velasco Cruz, "O porto do Rio de Janeiro no século XIX, *Revista Tempo* 8, August 1988, accessed October 20, 2015, http://www.historia.uff.br/tempo/artigos_livres/artg8-7.pdf.
4. "Evolution of the Population of the City of Rio de Janeiro 1872—2010," accessed January 27, 2016, http://www.censo2010.ibge.gov.br/sinopse/index.php?dados=6&uf=00

CHAPTER TWO

1. Maria Beltrão, "Os tupinambá no Rio de Janeiro," in *Anais do Museu Paulista: História e Cultura Material*, 238, accessed January 22, 2016, http://www.scielo.br/scielo.php?pid=S0101-47141993000100015&script=sci_arttext
2. Jean Marcel Carvalho França, Visões do Rio de Janeiro Colonial—antologia de textos 1531–1800 (Rio de Janeiro: EdUERJ, 1977); Pero Lopes de Sousa, *Diário de navegação de Pero Lopes de Souza: Estudo crítico pelo comandante Eugênio de Castro* (Rio de Janeiro: Edição da Comissão Brasileira de Centenários Portugueses,1940), 187–91.
3. Mary C. Karasch, *Slave Life in Rio de Janeiro, 1808–1850* (Princeton, NJ: Princeton University Press, 1987).
4. *Recueil des lois constitutives des colonies anglaises, confédérées sous la dénomination d'Etats-Unis de l'Amérique septentrionale, auquel on a joint les actes*

d'indépendance, de confédération et autres actes du congrès general, accessed January 22, 2016, https://books.google.com.br/books/about/Recueil_des_lois_constitu tives_des_colon.html?id=r4g7AAAAcAAJ&redir_esc=y

5. The original title in German was *Warhaftige Historia und beschreibung eyner Landtschafft der Wilden Nacketen, Grimmigen Menschfresser-Leuthen in der Newenwelt America gelegen* (Marpurg, 1557). Fundação Biblioteca Nacional, Rio de Janeiro, Brazil, accessed October 22, 2015, https://archive.org/details/staden

6. Alberto Costa e Silva, "Comprando e vendendo alcorões no Rio de Janeiro do século XIX." *Revista de Estudos Avançados* 18, no. 50, 285–384, http://dx.doi .org/10.1590/S0103-40142004000100024.

7. See Voyages, the Trans-Atlantic Slave Trade Database, accessed October 21, 2015, http://slavevoyages.org/voyage/.

CHAPTER THREE

1. Fernandes, Isabel Maria Fernandes, "Alimentos e alimentação no Portugal Quinhentista," accessed October 20, 2015, http://hdl.handle.net/1822/12471.

2. Rio de Janeiro, Population Evolution—1992–2010, Instituto Brasileiro de Geografia e Estatística, IBGE, http://cod.ibge.gov.br/234ZC.

3. A experiência da metrópole carioca como Estado da Guanabara (1960/75), accessed October 25, 2015, http://www.rio.rj.gov.br/dlstatic/10112/4205237/4101461/ quartas_angela_moulin_2006.pdf

4. Data from the site Bússola Escolar, accessed December 3, 2015 http://www .bussolaescolar.com.br/historia_do_brasil/imigracao_no_brasil.htm.

CHAPTER FOUR

1. Sir Joseph Banks, *The Endeavor Journal of Sir Joseph Banks, 1768–1771* (transcription at the University of Sidney Library), accessed November 16, 2015, http:// setis.library.usyd.edu.au/ozlit/pdf/p00021.pdf 39.

2. Carta a João Rodrigues de Macedo enviando o recibo dos gêneros a serem comprados e remetidos a capitania de Minas Gerais (Rio de Janeiro: Coleção Casa dos Contos, Fundação Biblioteca Nacional), original manuscript of July 1778.

3. *O Cozinheiro Nacional*, 5th ed (Rio de Janeiro: H. Garnier Livreiro-Editor, 1899), 157–274.

CHAPTER SIX

1. *Livro de Cozinha da Infanta D. Maria*, Códice Português I. E. 33., da Biblioteca Nacional de Nápoles (Lisboa: Imprensa Nacional—Casa da Moeda, 1986), recipe 6, 13.

2. *Livro de Cozinha da Infanta D. Maria*, recipe 6, 4.

3. Domingos Rodrigues, *A arte de cozinha* (Lisboa: na Offic. da viúva de Lino da Silva Godinho, 1821), recipe 4, 13.

4. Maria de Lourdes Modesto, *Cozinha tradicional portuguesa* (Lisboa: Verbo,1982).

5. Recipe from Maria Thereza Costa, *Noções de Arte Culinária*, 7th ed. (São Paulo, 1921).

6. Costa, *Noções de Arte Culinária*, p. 183.

7. Helena B. Sangirardi, *A alegria de cozinhar* (São Paulo: Livraria Prado Ltda., 1954), 531.

Bibliography

Agassiz, Elizabeth Cabot, and Louis Agassiz. *A Journey in Brazil*. Boston: Ticknor and Fields, 1868.

Albala, Ken. *The Banquet: Dining in the Great Courts of Late Renaissance Europe*. Urbana: University of Illinois Press, 2007.

Alencastro, Luiz Felipe, ed., *História da vida privada no Brasil*, vol. 2. São Paulo: Companhia das Letras, 1997.

Cardim, Fernão. *Tratados da gente e terra do Brasil*. Edited by Ana Maria de Azevedo. São Paulo: Hedra, 2009.

Cascudo, Luis da Camara. *História da alimentação no Brasil*. Vols. 1 and 2. Belo Horizonte: Editora Itatiaia, 1983.

Cavalcanti, Nireu. *O Rio de Janeiro setecentista: A vida e a construção da cidade da invasão francesa até a chegada da corte*. Rio de Janeiro: Jorge Zahar Editor, 2004.

Certeau, Michel, Luce Giard, and Pierre Mayol. *L'invention du quotidien, 2. Habiter, cuisiner*. Collection Folio Essais 146. Paris: Gallimard, 1994.

Chastanet, M., F.-X. Fauvelle-Aymar, and D. Juhé-Beaulaton. *Cuisine et société en Afrique: Histoire, saveurs, savoir-faire*. Paris: Éditions Karthala, 2002.

Coe, Sophie D., *America's First Cuisines*. Austin: University of Texas Press, 1994.

Cruz, Maria Cecília Velasco. "O porto do Rio de Janeiro no século XIX." *Revista Tempo* 8 (August 1988). Accessed October 20, 2015. http://www.historia.uff.br/tempo/artigos_livres/artg8-7.pdf

Cunha, Manoela Carneiro da. *Negros estrangeiros, os escravos libertos e sua volta à África*. São Paulo: Companhia das Letras, 2012.

DaMatta, Roberto. *Carnival, Rogues, and Heroes: An Interpretation of the Brazilian Dilemma*. Translated by John Drury. Notre Dame, IN: Helen Kellog Institute of International Studies, 1991.

Davis, Natalie Zemon. *Society and Culture in Early Modern France*. Stanford, CA: Stanford University Press, 1975.

Disney, A. R. *A History of Portugal and the Portuguese Empire, from Beginnings to 1807: Portugal*. Vol. 1. New York: Cambridge University Press, 2009.

Elsner, Jás, and Joan-Pau Rubiés, eds. *Voyages and Visions, towards a Cultural History of Travel*. London: Reaktion Books, 1999.

Fernandes, Isabel Maria. "Alimentos e alimentação no Portugal Quinhentista." *Revista de Guimarães* 112: 125–215. Accessed October 20, 2015. http://repositorium .sdum.uminho.pt/handle/1822/12471

Flandrin, Jeand Louis, and Massimo Montanarini. *Food: A Culinary History*. Translated by Albert Sonnenfeld. New York: Penguin Books, 2000.

"Francisco de Melo Palheta e a história do café no Brasil, carta régia de 16 de fevereiro de 1734." *Jangada Brasil*. Accessed October 20, 2015. http://www.jangadab rasil.com.br/novembro15/of15110c.htm

Freyre, Gilberto. *Assucar*. Rio de Janeiro: José Olympio, 1939.

Fridman, Fania. *Donos do Rio em nome do Rei*. Rio de Janeiro: Jorge Zahar Editor, 1999.

Gay, Peter, *The Education of the Senses: The Bourgeois Experience: Victoria to Freud*. New York: W. W. Norton, 1984.

Heers, Jacques. *Fêtes, jeux et joutes dans les sociétes d'Occident à la fin du Moyen-Âge*. Paris: Librairie J.Vrin, 1977.

Horta, Nina, *Não é sopa, crônicas e receitas de comida*. São Paulo: Companhia das Letras, 1995.

Instituto Brasileiro de Geografia e Estatística (IBGE). "Evolution of the Population of the City of Rio de Janeiro 1872–2010." Sinopse do Censo Demográfico 2010. Accessed October 20, 2015. http://www.censo2010.ibge.gov.br/sinopse/index.php? dados=6&uf=00

Kagan, Richard L., and Phillip D. Morgan, eds. *Atlantic Diasporas: Jews, Conversos, and Crypto-Jews in the Age of Mercantilism, 1500–1800*. Baltimore: Johns Hopkins University Press, 2009.

Karasch, Mary C., *Slave Life in Rio de Janeiro, 1808–1850*. Princeton, NJ: Princeton University Press, 1987.

Knox, E. L. Skip. "The Population of Early Modern Europe." *Europe in the Age of Reformation*. Accessed October 20, 2015. https://europeanhistory.boisestate.edu/ reformation/society/population.shtml.

Lery, Jean de. *Histoire d'un voyage fait en la terre du Bresil, autrement dite Amerique*. La Rochelle: pour Antoine Chupin, 1578. Biblioteca Nacional de Portugal. Accessed October 10, 2018. http://purl.pt/136.

Macdonald, Janet. *Feeding Nelson's Navy: The True Story of Food at Sea in the Georgian Era*. London: Chatham Publishing, 2006.

Melammed, Renée Levine. *A Question of Identity: Iberian Conversos in Historical Perspective*. Oxford: Oxford University Press, 2004.

Palla, Maria José. *Banquets et manières de table au Moyen Âge*. Aix-en-Provence: Presses universitaires de Provence, 1996. Accessed October 28, 2015, http://books .openedition.org/pup/3542.

Queiroz Mattoso, Kátia, *Ser escravo no Brasil*. São Paulo: Editora Brasiliense, 1982.

Recueil des lois constitutives des colonies anglaises, confédérées sous la dénomination d'Etats-Unis de l'Amérique septentrionale, auquel on a joint les actes d'indépendance, de confédération et autres actes du congrès général. Philadelphia, 1778. Accessed October 28, 2015. goo.gl/7fOie2

Schiebinger, Londa. *Plants and Empire: Colonial Bioprospecting in the Atlantic World.* Cambridge, MA: Harvard University Press, 2004.

Schiebinger, Londa, and Claudia Swan, eds. *Colonial Botany, Science, Commerce and Politics in the Early Modern World.* Philadelphia: University of Pennsylvania Press, 2005.

Silva, Alberto Costa e. "Comprando e vendendo Alcorões no Rio de Janeiro do século XIX." *Revista Estudos Avançados* 18, no. 50 (2004): 285–93.

Staden, Hans. *Warhaftige Historia vnd beschreibung eyner Landtschafft der Wilden, Nacketen, Grimmigen Menschfresser Leuthen, in der Newenwelt America.* Marpurg, 1557. Coleção Brasiliana—José e Guita Mindlin. Accessed March 17, 2015. http://www.brasiliana.usp.br/bbd/handle/1918/06000100

Thévet, André. *Les singularitez de la France Antarctique, autrement nommée Amerique, & de plusieurs Terres & Isles decouvertes de nostre temps.* Paris: chez ler heritiers de Maurice de la Porte, 1558. Biblioteca Brasiliana Guita e José Mindlin. Accessed October 29, 2015. http://www.brasiliana.usp.br/bbd/handle/1918/01918600

Tinhorão, José Ramos. *As festas no Brasil colonial.* São Paulo: Editora 34, 2000.

Todorov, Tzvetan. *La conquête de l'Amérique.* Paris: Éditions du Seuil, 1982.

Ventura, Roberto. *Casa-grande e senzala, coleção Folha Explica.* São Paulo: Publifolha, 2000.

HISTORIC COOKBOOKS

Arte nova, e curiosa para conserveiros e copeiros e mais pessoas que se ocupao em fazer doces, e conservas com frutas de varias qualidades, e outras mais receitas particulares que pertencem a mesma arte. Lisboa: Officina de José de Aquino Bulhoens, 1788.

Artusi, Pellegrino. *La scienza in cucina e l'arte di magiar bene.* Florence: Casa Editrice Marzocco, 1954.

Breteuil, Julio, *Novo cozinheiro universal, contendo as melhores receitas das cozinhas francezas e estrangeiras e numerosas receitas brasileiras.* Rio de Janeiro: H. Garnier, 1901.

Caramel, Blanche. *Le nouveau livre de cuisine.* Paris: Éditions Gautier-Languereau, 1927.

Costa, Maria Thereza A., *Noções de arte culinária.* São Paulo: Augusto Siqueira e Comp., 1921.

Doceiro Nacional ou a arte de fazer toda a qualidade de doces. Rio de Janeiro: B. L. Garnier, Livreiro-Editor, 1895. Accessed November 1, 2015. http://www.brasiliana.usp.br/bbd/handle/1918/00655700

Lima, Constança Oliva de. *Doceira Brasileira.* Rio de Janeiro: Laemmert & Co, 1896.

Livro de Cozinha da Infanta D. Maria. C, códice português I. E. 33., da Biblioteca Nacional de Nápoles. Lisboa: Imprensa Nacional—Casa da Moeda, 1986.

Maria, Rosa. *A arte de comer bem.* Rio de Janeiro: H. Leonardos Editor, 1936.

Modesto, Maria de Lourdes, *Cozinha tradicional portuguesa.* Lisboa: Verbo, 1983.

O cozinheiro nacional, 5th ed. Rio de Janeiro: H. Garnier, Livreiro-Editor, 1899.

Paranhos, Myrthes. *Receitas culinárias*. Rio de Janeiro: Letras e Artes, 1962.

R.C.M. *O cozinheiro imperial*. Facsimile of the second edition of 1843. São Paulo: Editora Nova Cultural, 1996.

Rodrigues, Domingos. *A arte de cozinha*. Lisboa: na Offic. da viúva de Lino da Silva Godinho, 1821. First edition from 1680. Biblioteca Nacional de Lisboa. Accessed October 29, 2015. http://purl.pt/17017

Sangirardi, Helena B. *A alegria de cozinhar*. São Paulo: Livraria Prado Ltda., 1954.

Um tratado da cozinha Portuguesa no século XV. Manuscript transcription by the Fundação Biblioteca Nacional, Rio de Janeiro. Accessed October 29, 2015. http://www.dominiopublico.gov.br/download/texto/bn000109.pdf

BOOKS BY THE AUTHOR

Zoladz, Marcia. *Passeios e sabores cariocas. A combinação deliciosa de um guia turístico e um livro de receitas*. Rio de Janeiro: Casa da Palavra, 2014.

———. *Sobremesas e doces brasileiros*. São Paulo: V&R Editores, 2013.

———. *Brigadeiros e Bolinhas doces e salgados*. São Paulo: Publifolha, 2011.

———. Das Männerkochbuch, e-book. 1st edition, 2015. Print edition Franfurt: Fischer Verlag, 1997.

———. *Portugiesisch Kochbuch, Geschischte und ihre Gerichte*, Berlin: Edition diá/ Verlag Die Werkstatt, 2004.

Index

About the Author

Marcia Zoladz is a cookbook author and journalist and currently lives in São Paulo. She was born and raised in Rio de Janeiro, with frequent visits to France, and did part of her college studies in the United States. She has published four books with recipes and their stories, and is published in Germany, Holland, Brazil, and the United States. As a food historian, Zoladz is an active member of the Oxford Symposium on Food and Cookery, an open-minded yearly event held in Oxford, England.